SCANDIKITCHEN
Midsommar
Simply delicious food for summer days

SCANDIKITCHEN

Midsommar

Simply delicious food for summer days

BRONTË AURELL

Photography by Peter Cassidy

RYLAND PETERS & SMALL
LONDON • NEW YORK

DEDICATION
For Astrid, Elsa and Jonas –
with all my love, always xxx

SENIOR DESIGNER
Sonya Nathoo

COMMISSIONING EDITOR
Alice Sambrook

HEAD OF PRODUCTION
Patricia Harrington

ART DIRECTOR
Leslie Harrington

EDITORIAL DIRECTOR
Julia Charles

PUBLISHER
Cindy Richards

FOOD STYLIST
Kathy Kordalis

PROP STYLIST
Tony Hutchinson

RECIPE TESTER
Cathy Seward

INDEXER
Vanessa Bird

Recipe contributions:
Kobi Ruzicka: Curried
Cauliflower & Rye Grain Salad
(page 62), Birgitte Agger Mote:
Buttermilk Panna Cotta (page
152), Jon Anders Fjeldsrud:
Aquavit Cocktails (page 172)

Naturally hand-dyed fabrics
by Isabella Strambio
www.twome.co.uk

Edible flowers and speciality
ingredients by the lovely
people at Eurofrutta
www.eurofrutta.co.uk

Originally published as
ScandiKitchen Summer in 2018.
This edition published in 2021
by Ryland Peters & Small
20–21 Jockey's Fields
London WC1R 4BW
and
Ryland Peters & Small, Ltd.
341 E 116th St
New York NY 10029
www.rylandpeters.com

Text © Brontë Aurell 2018, 2021

Design and commissioned photographs
© Ryland Peters & Small 2018, 2021

ISBN: 978-1-78879-357-5

10 9 8 7 6 5 4 3 2 1

Printed and bound in China.

CIP data from the Library of Congress
has been applied for. A CIP record for
this book is available from the British
Library.

Photography credits
All photography by Peter Cassidy apart
from pages:

4–5 photo division/Getty Images
46–47 Danita Delimont/Getty Images
104–105 Johner Images/Getty Images
126 Ragnar Singsaas/WireImage/Getty Images
127al Christophe Boisvieux/Getty Images
127cl Franz Aberham/Getty Images
127r Tolga Akmen/Anadolu Agency/Getty Images
160–161 Johner Images/Getty Images
174–175 Lilly Husbands/Getty Images

NOTES
* Both British (metric) and
American (imperial plus US cups)
measurements are included in these
recipes; however, it is important to work
with one set of measurements and not
alternate between the two within a recipe.
* All butter is salted unless specified.
* All eggs are medium (UK) or large
(US), unless specified as large, in which
case US extra-large should be used.
Uncooked or partially cooked eggs should
not be served to the very old, frail, young
children, pregnant women or those with
compromised immune systems.
* Ovens should be preheated to the
specified temperatures. We recommend
using an oven thermometer. If using
a fan-assisted oven, adjust temperatures
according to the manufacturer's
instructions.
* When a recipe calls for the grated zest
of citrus fruit, buy unwaxed fruit and wash
well before using. If you can only find
treated fruit, scrub well in warm soapy
water before using.
* Always check that flowers used for
garnish are food-safe and pesticide-free.

CONTENTS

Introduction

The Scandinavian year is one of stark contrasts. It's often portrayed as the cold north, full of snow and darkness – which is actually true, for a few months. But after the darkness follows the light. When the snow finally melts and the days are once again lit by the sun, we Scandinavians wake up with a force of energy, ready to appreciate everything nature has to offer. No sooner have we packed up our skis and heavy coats than we're out hiking, cycling, having picnics and sitting in our gardens enjoying every moment outdoors.

In the fourteen years since my husband Jonas and I opened our shop and café, ScandiKitchen, in central London, we have learned how people from other nations view us and our habits. We celebrate all the Scandinavian seasons at the café in true style – so in the first few years of being open we had lots of curious locals stop by to witness us wearing the midsummer flowers in our hair, eating herring, singing at the tops of our voices and dancing around a midsummer pole. Now, many of those customers join in our summer celebrations – even getting into the spirit of things at our crayfish parties which mark the last 'hurrah' at the end of the warm months.

Part of what makes the Scandinavian summer magical is the intense energy we seem to find within ourselves. In contrast to the calm and slowness of our winter, the summer is busy, intense and full of promise.

Understanding the concept of lagom (not too much, not too little, but just right) is to appreciate that the spirit of our countries is based around ensuring that everything we do is in balance. The stereotype is generally true: excess is limited in Scandinavia. We are practical in our approach to anything, from design, furniture and homes, to how we live and what we eat. Yes, we love cake, but we balance it out with fresh salads. If we enjoy a heavy lunch, we have a light dinner. Open sandwiches on fibre-rich rye bread means we don't skimp on the mayo.

This isn't a diet book. I don't subscribe to the idea of restrictive eating, and I don't think that would be a true representation of how Scandinavians really eat. We devour the summer months and celebrate them as much as we can, so of course there's going to be cakes and treats. The recipes in this book will produce good food with respect to both tradition and modern trends in healthy eating. I've included plenty of indulgent cakes and bakes, as well as salads and a few leaner dinners. This is how I eat, with lagom, and for the love of good food.

Brontë x

The Scandinavian Summer Pantry

Across a landmass that stretches from the flat lands of Denmark to the rocky fjells of northern Norway, our fields and forests are varied and plentiful and our store cupboards are diverse. The summer months across Norway, Sweden and Denmark are full of light, which produces an abundance of colourful produce. Our fields are green and lush, our berries plump and bright. Here are some of the most common ingredients we use in our cooking over the summer months.

BERRIES

Cloudberries/multebær/hjortron

Found in the wild and very hard to cultivate artificially, these orange berries (which look a bit like plump orange raspberries) grow on stalks. In North America, they are often referred to as 'bakeapples'. They can't be picked by machine, only by hand, and even this can be tricky – most burst when picked. The cloudberry season is only around three weeks long. For all these reasons, this delicious berry is expensive and hard to get hold of, so most commonly, we use a cloudberry jam/jelly or frozen berries. If you know of a cloudberry patch in a forest, keep it to yourself. These berries pair very well with the flavours of apple, vanilla and strong cheeses. If you need to replace in a recipe, a tart raspberry is the closest ingredient in taste.

Lingonberries/tyttebær/lingon

This is a little red, tart berry found in abundance in Sweden, Norway and Finland. From the same family as cranberries, the tartness lends itself well to being served with meat (it is most famously served with meatballs). Lingonberries can also be used in cookies and cakes – pair them with something quite sweet if you use the frozen or fresh ones as they are really quite sharp in flavour. If you cannot get hold of lingonberries, substitute with raspberries (for sweet recipes) or cranberries (for more savoury dishes).

Strawberries/jordbær/jordgubb

We have two varieties of strawberries: the normal ones from the garden, available in all shops – and then the little wild strawberries. The latter can be found in Norwegian and Swedish forests towards the end of July. Wild strawberries are very sweet, small berries (often less than 1 cm/¼ inch long). If you have ever tasted wild strawberries yourself, you will know that they are utterly delicious.

Blueberries/blåbær/blåbär

The type of blueberries you buy in the shop are called blueberries, of course. The type of blueberries you find in the wild all over northern Scandinavia we also call 'blåbär', but in English, these are actually known as bilberries. Wild blueberries or bilberries have a delicious sweet flavour and are a lot smaller. If you can get them then go for them – they are a deep blue colour even inside. Bilberries can be bought frozen from speciality shops or online.

Elderberries (elderflower)/hyldebær/blomst/fläder

In Scandinavia, elderflower is used mostly in jams/

jellies, cordials and cakes. The Elderberry is also used a lot in Denmark to make elderberry cordial – a strong-tasting drink which is full of vitamins.

VEGETABLES

Beetroot (beet)/rødbeder/rödbetor
Used pickled, cooked and raw, this vegetable is a real staple of Scandinavian food, in everything from salads to dips or hot dishes. If you use a store-bought beetroot/beet pickle, do check if it's filled with sweeteners. Eastern European and Scandinavian versions tend not to be and therefore give a better result, in my opinion.

Nettles/brændnælder/nässel
Fresh nettles have an earthy taste similar to spinach, but with a coarser texture and stronger after-taste. Make sure you wear gloves for foraging and pick only the new top leaves in spring time – nettles in late summer tend to be harsh and tough. Boiling them in water for 2 minutes before using them will kill the stings. Dried nettles are a good, easy option and can be bought online and added to salads or crackers or used as a general flavouring like dried herbs.

Wild mushrooms/champignons/svamp
The autumn/fall is usually the time for foraging for fresh mushrooms – and we like to use fresh whenever we can. During other seasons we use a lot of dried mushrooms, most often the Swedish 'Kantareller' (chanterelles) or 'Karl Johan' (porcini).

HERBS AND SPICES

Cinnamon/kanel
Some cheaper varieties of cinnamon are made from an inferior type of bark, called 'cassia bark', which contains high levels of coumarin that is not good for you in large doses. If you can, go for high grade ceylon bark cinnamon instead, which has lower levels of coumarin and a better flavour.

Vanilla/vanilje
Most Scandinavian cookbooks will call for vanilla sugar, which is a quick and easy substitute for whole vanilla pods/beans. You can buy this in Scandinavian food shops, or make your own at home by grinding together 275 g/2 cups of icing/confectioners' sugar with 2 dried vanilla pods/beans in a food processor or spice grinder until the pods are pulverized. Sift to remove the woody bits and use as needed. You can normally just substitute with vanilla extract or vanilla pods/beans too.

Cardamom/kardemumma
Vikings first brought this spice back from their raids on Constantinople. We use it a lot in baking recipes, including the dough for our buns. For maximum flavour, you can buy the whole shelled seeds online and grind them yourself using a spice grinder.

Salt
Scandinavians have been preserving food in salt for centuries, and it turns out we have a love for

anything salty – from well-seasoned savoury dishes, to sprinkling it on cookies or cakes.

Liquorice/lakrids/lakrits

The Finns became hooked on the flavour of liquorice, used in a lot of cough medicine, at the turn of the 19th century. Someone had the bright idea to add the flavour to sweets, and from then ammonium chloride began to be added in greater quantities (this is the salty flavour also known as 'salmiakki'). The salty flavour in Scandinavian liquorice is now so strong that most non-Scandinavians can't eat it. Although, if you become hooked on the acquired taste, you will need the stronger stuff. Use as a syrup or powder in cakes, meringues or ice creams.

Dill

We use dill a lot throughout the summer months to give a lift to salads, fish or even chicken dishes. For crayfish served at crayfish parties we use crown dill for its strong flavour – which is dill that has been allowed to flower. It is quite hard to get hold of outside Sweden, but you can always grow your own or use normal fresh dill instead.

OILS, VINEGARS & MUSTARDS

24% Vinegar/ättika/eddike

A very strong pickling vinegar, this needs to be diluted to the strength required for what you need to use it for. It is usually 5–6% for veg and 12% for herring or other cured fish.

Rapeseed oil/rapsolie/rapsolja

Healthy rapeseed oil is popular all over Scandinavia and has found fame in other countries. However, not all rapeseed oils are created equal and an inferior one won't do your dish any favours, so always use the best-quality oil can find, whether it's olive or rapeseed.

Mustard/sennep/senap

We favour sweet, strong mustards. You can substitute with a grainy Dijon, although in some recipes you may need to add a pinch of sugar, too.

YEAST AND LEAVENERS

Fresh yeast/gær/jäst

25 g/1 oz. fresh compressed yeast is equivalent to 13 g/$2^1/2$ teaspoons of active dry yeast granules. Instant dried yeast sachets are also an option – follow the guidelines on sachets for dosage and always add these to the dry ingredients. Note that liquid over 36–37°C (97-99°F) will kill fresh yeast – as will salt added directly to the yeast.

FLOURS AND GRAINS

Rye flour/rugmel/rågmjöl

You can't work your way through Scandinavian food without encountering rye flour. White rye flour is milled without the outside shell and loses most of its goodness, so I tend to use the wholegrain variety. While you can't replace wheat for rye, you can experiment with replacing 10% of the white flour, then a little more next time.

Spelt flour/speltmel/dinkelmjöl

An older variety of wheat grain which is less refined. The white variety is milled without the outer husk and is more refined, so again I would go for the wholegrain variety if you're using it for health reasons.

Rye flakes/rugflager/rågflingor

Give a more wholesome bite and taste to granola, flapjacks and porridge. If it's a bit too wholesome for your taste, use half oats and half rye flakes.

Rye kernels (rye berries)/rugkerner/rågkärna

There are two kinds on the market – the whole rye kernel and the kibbled one. You need the whole one if boiling for salads etc. – and the kibbled one is essential when making good rye bread (see page 149), where the whole one would be too hard to use. If you can only get the whole variety, you can chop the rye kernels in a food processor with a few quick pulses (not too much – you only just want to cut them in half).

Malt

You can buy barley malt protein powder or syrup online. We also sometimes use a low-alcohol malt beer in our rye bread dough.

Oats/havre

We tend to use a lot of cut oats or jumbo rolled oats – we rarely use the finely-ground oatmeal.

Crispbread/knækbrød/knäckebröd/knekkebrød

Not a flour or grain, but such an important part of our store-cupboard that it needs to be mentioned, as they are on the dining table for most meals, especially breakfast. A good homemade crispbread is made with rye, water, yeast and a little salt. You can use my recipe on page 143 or buy them from Scandinavian food shops. It takes a lot of drying in a warm oven to get the homemade ones nearly as crisp as the store-bought ones, as the professional bakers use really hot ovens heated to 400°C (750°F).

DRINKS

Aquavit

A grain-based alcoholic drink, flavoured with herbs and spices. Most people often enjoy as part of a smörgåsbord or with pickled herring or crayfish. See my recipes for easy versions of dill and fennel-flavoured aquavit on page 171.

OTHER

Buttermilk/kærnemælk

In Danish cuisine, buttermilk often makes an appearance – especially in the summer dish 'koldskål' (see page 152). I like using buttermilk in batters for pancakes and in cakes – it has sour notes and is very fresh tasting for summer.

Marzipan

We use a lot of marzipan in baking but never the cheap kind which has a low almond content – go for 50% almond content as a minimum, or make your own (unless you're using it to cover a cake).

breakfast & brunch

As the days get lighter, I long for my parents' cottage by the sea. Mostly because I savour eating breakfast there outdoors, while listening to the wind in the trees and the waves crashing onto the shore in the distance. As my family gather around the table and talk excitedly about the day ahead, I always feel that there is something magical about eating in the fresh air first thing in the morning. It wakes you up with its (often broken) gentle promises of sunshine and warmth. We plan the day ahead – on the beach or hiking – while savouring the young sunrays and hoping they will last the day!

Rye & Banana Bread

At our café, people used to ask for banana bread a lot. As it's not really a traditional Scandinavian thing, we wanted to make it our own with a Scandi twist. So, we created this version with rye flour to make it more wholesome. We like to serve it with a delicious cinnamon butter, that just melts on toasted slices of this loaf.

4 very ripe bananas

100 g/scant ½ cup Greek/plain Greek-style yogurt

1 tablespoon lemon juice

1 teaspoon vanilla extract or vanilla sugar

125 g/1 cup minus 1 tablespoon plain/all-purpose flour

125 g/1 generous cup wholemeal/ wholewheat rye flour

½ teaspoon salt

1 teaspoon bicarbonate of soda/ baking soda

125 g/1⅛ sticks butter, softened

150 g/¾ cup dark brown soft sugar

2 UK large/US extra-large eggs

cinnamon butter, to serve (optional)

500 g/1 lb. loaf pan, lined with non-stick baking parchment

Makes 1 loaf

Preheat the oven to 180°C (350°F) Gas 4.

Mash the bananas and mix with the yogurt, lemon juice and vanilla and set aside.

Mix the flours with the salt and bicarbonate of soda/baking soda and set aside.

Cream together the butter and dark brown soft sugar in a stand mixer fitted with the paddle attachment, or using a hand-held electric whisk. Add the eggs, one at a time, scraping down the sides of the bowl between each addition to ensure they are fully incorporated.

Add the mashed banana mixture and mix until incorporated, then add the flours and mix briefly until smooth. Do not over-mix.

Spoon the mixture into the lined loaf pan. Bake in the middle of the preheated oven for around 30 minutes, or until a skewer inserted into the middle comes out just clean. Leave to cool a little before turning out of the pan. Cut into slices and serve toasted, with plenty of cinnamon butter (see below).

Cinnamon butter

Mix three tablespoons of strong cinnamon sugar (ratio 1:3) with half a packet of soft unsalted butter – re-chill and use as needed.

Rye & Oat Pancakes

I love fluffy white pancakes as much as the next person – but I am not a massive wheat fan and I try to find alternatives where I can. These rye flour pancakes have a deliciously nutty aftertaste. Yes, my kids get the ones with added chocolate and they love them. If you are not including the chocolate, then serve these wholesome pancakes with fresh berry compote and plain yogurt.

50 g/⅓ cup steel-cut oats/medium oatmeal
200 ml/generous ¾ cup buttermilk
100 g/1 scant cup rye flour
½ teaspoon salt
2 tablespoons caster/ granulated sugar
1 teaspoon baking powder
½ teaspoon bicarbonate of soda/baking soda
2 eggs
75 g/½ cup chocolate chips (optional)
butter, for frying

Makes 6–7 pancakes

Add the steel-cut oats or oatmeal to the buttermilk and leave to soak for at least 10 minutes.

Meanwhile, mix the dry ingredients together in a bowl.

Separate the eggs and mix the yolks into the flour mixture. Add the buttermilk and oats and stir until incorporated. A few lumps are fine – it is best not to over-mix. Stir in the chocolate chips (if using).

In a clean bowl, whisk the egg whites using a hand-held electric whisk until soft peaks form. Carefully fold the whites into the batter, trying not to knock out the air.

Heat a small knob/pat of butter on a frying pan/skillet over a medium heat. Drop in spoonfuls of batter to make pancakes of around 10 cm/4 inches in diameter. Fry in batches, depending on the size of your pan, for about 1 minute on each side until golden. Note that rye flour takes a little longer to cook – so be patient.

Crispy Wholemeal Waffles

Scandinavians love waffles; Norwegians especially. We use a heart-shaped waffle iron, now available across the world from online retailers. Do invest in a good one – they last forever and you will use it a lot once you get into weekly waffle making. Waffles are a delicious treat. If you remove all the fat, you end up with – in my opinion – quite boring waffles. Boring is not why waffles were invented, so I've left in some butter – because, well, butter isn't that bad for you as long as you don't overdo it.

100 g/1 stick minus 1 tablespoon butter, melted, plus extra for brushing
175 g/1⅓ cups wholemeal/ wholewheat flour
175 g/1⅓ cups plain/ all-purpose flour
2 teaspoons baking powder
pinch of salt
½ teaspoon ground cardamom
½ teaspoon vanilla extract
250 ml/generous 1 cup buttermilk
250 ml/1 cup plus 1 tablespoon water
1 egg
2 teaspoons chia seeds and 1 small grated apple (optional)

heart-shaped waffle iron

Makes about 6 waffles

Preheat the waffle iron and brush with melted butter.

Mix together all the ingredients to form a smooth batter. If you want to add the chia seeds and apple, do this right at the end before you make the waffles.

Add a ladleful of batter to the preheated waffle iron and close the lid. Leave to cook for 2–3 minutes or until golden and crispy.

Remove from the waffle iron and serve immediately (or they go soggy). Repeat with remaining batter. Serve with summer fruit and yogurt – or just on their own.

Swedish Plätt Pancakes

Plättar are little pancakes. In Sweden, these mini pancakes are eaten as a dessert, often with cold stirred lingonberries (see page 101), or lingonberry jam/jelly, but I think they make a brilliant brunch too. Because they have no raising agent, they are flat like French crêpes, rather than fluffy like American-style pancakes. However, I like the addition of a glug of beer to the batter just before frying, as I find the carbonated liquid gives the pancakes a little lift. You can leave this out and replace with a little more milk or a dash of sparkling water instead, if you prefer. Some people fry their plättar in a special pan (like the one pictured) with large blini-sized shallow round indents of around 8 cm/3 inches across. You can, of course, make them freestyle on a normal pan/skillet too, but they will not be as uniform. If you have metal cookie cutters, you could drop the batter inside these for a neater finish.

175 g/1⅓ cups plain/all-purpose flour
pinch of ground cardamom
1 tablespoon icing/confectioners'
   sugar
pinch of salt
3 eggs
500 ml/2 cups plus 2 tablespoons
   whole milk
25 g/1¾ tablespoons butter, melted
50 ml/3½ tablespoons beer (lager)
extra butter and olive oil, for frying
Cold Stirred Lingonberries (see
   page 101) or lingonberry jam/jelly,
   to serve (optional)

Serves 3–4

In a large mixing bowl, stir together the flour with the cardamom, icing/confectioners' sugar and salt. Add the eggs and mix until smooth. Whisk in the milk, bit by bit, stirring after each addition to avoid lumps. Whisk in the melted butter. Leave the batter to stand at room temperature for 30 minutes.

Just before you want to fry your pancakes, add the beer. Give a brief stir but don't over-mix.

Preheat the pan over a medium heat and add a little butter and oil. Drop in spoonfuls of the batter and fry briefly, turning once, until golden on both sides. Serve the pancakes hot, with a large helping of cold stirred lingonberries or lingonberry jam/jelly.

Coconut Granola for Elsa & Astrid

There are a million versions of coconut granola on the internet –
I am certainly not the inventor of granola! What makes this one
different is that I pack in as many nutritious ingredients as I can
– and maybe because kids love cereal, mine suddenly don't seem to
notice how many different seeds they are eating. The original recipe
came to me via my sister, and this adapted version is the one we
have on the breakfast table in the Aurell household in London.

75 g/generous ⅓ cup coconut oil
2 generous tablespoons good
   quality honey
2 tablespoons date syrup
   (optional)
1 tablespoon dark brown soft
   sugar (optional)
seeds from half a vanilla pod/bean
   or 1 teaspoon vanilla sugar
1 teaspoon ground cinnamon
100 g/generous 1 cup jumbo rolled
   oats with 50 g/½ cup rye flakes
   OR just 150 g/generous 1½ cups
   jumbo rolled oats

75 g/1¼ cups large coconut
   flakes
50 g/½ cup roughly chopped
   almonds
50 g/½ cup roughly chopped
   hazelnuts
50 g/⅓ cup pumpkin seeds
50 g/⅓ cup linseeds (flaxseeds)
50 g/⅓ cup sunflower seeds
50 g/⅓ cup sesame seeds

*Makes enough to keep
a family of four in granola
for a good week*

Preheat the oven to 160°C (325°F) Gas 3.

Put the coconut oil, honey, syrup and sugar (if using), vanilla and
cinnamon in a large oven tray and warm over a low heat, until melted
together and hot but not smoking.

Mix together the rest of the dry ingredients, then add them to the tray
of hot oil and mix well.

Level the mixture and bake in the preheated oven for about 20 minutes –
checking and stirring every 5 minutes. The granola is ready when it has
turned a deep golden colour – it will go stale more quickly if the mixture
is underbaked but don't allow it to go dark brown or it will taste burnt.

Remove the tray from the oven and leave the granola to cool, giving
it a shake once in a while to stop clumping. You can add dried fruits
to the cooled mixture at this point for a nice variation, if you like.

The granola will keep in a dry airtight container for several weeks.

Scandinavian brunch

The Scandinavian dining experience is often centred around sharing lots of small dishes – and brunch is no different. I just love getting people together and serving a little bit of what everyone fancies.

Scandinavians don't tend to skip breakfast. This is a fact, at least as far as the people that I know are concerned. While you probably will find Scandinavians who skip that first meal of the day, they are – in my experience – the exception rather than the rule.

Just like a smörgåsbord, a good Scandinavian brunch includes lots of little plates of delicious dishes, shared around on a big table. We sometimes do special brunch events at the café on weekends and they are always a big

hit. I think this is because a sharing-style breakfast gives you a little bit of everything you fancy, while still allowing you to keep in mind the Swedish principles of lagom: not too much, not too little.

Throughout the weekdays, Scandinavians tend to eat lighter things such as soured milk, oats and muesli – and, of course, a lot of crisp and rye breads. Rarely do we eat pastries or sweet treats on a weekday – but the weekends are an entirely different thing. It's all about

Real summer hygge sets in when we are just sitting down, talking and sharing food – time stops and life seems almost perfect.

balance and eating to suit the day we're having, whether it's a quick breakfast on a sensible Tuesday or a long, lazy brunch on a Sunday with family or friends. It's one of my favourite things about the summer months when I go back to see family in Denmark – everybody gets up, my dad will pop over to the bakers to get some locally baked fresh pastries and a loaf of rye bread, and we all help to arrange a huge table of sharing platters on the terrace. Real summer hygge sets in when we are just sitting down, talking and sharing food – time stops and life seems almost perfect.

When assembling a Scandinavian brunch, you can include everything from small pastries to fruit salad, fresh berries, soured milk or skyr with granola, rye and

crispbreads or crusty breakfast rolls. Perhaps you will add some warm Scandinavian sausages on the side, sliced cold meats or crisp streaky bacon (never back bacon), some smoked salmon or a selection of good cheeses. I always add a bowl of scrambled eggs to the table for people to help themselves, or boiled eggs with Kalles Kaviar (creamed smoked cod roe paste, a Swedish classic). Finish it off with a selection of jams/jellies and honey and you have a feast with plenty of lighter, fresh elements that can last you well into the afternoon.

It's all about having a spoon of this, a cup of that and another slice of what you fancy, while spending time with people you love. Preferably outside, in a light summer breeze, with a day of doing nothing ahead.

Pearl Barley Breakfast Pots

Cold pearl barley for breakfast is surprisingly filling and a great alternative to porridge. If you, like me, like to snack on nuts and seeds, then almonds probably feature on your list – they are delicious and full of goodness. I like to soak my almonds for 24 hours before using; it sounds like a faff, but it changes the whole taste and makes them much easier to digest. Simply pop your whole almonds in water, leave for 24 hours, then rinse and keep in the fridge for 3–4 days, using as needed. As for dried berries, if you soak these in black Earl Grey tea overnight, they become plump and juicy. Just give a quick rinse before using and then keep in the fridge for a few days.

4 tablespoons cold cooked pearl barley (see Note below)
150 ml/³⁄₄ cup yogurt of your choice
handful of soaked almonds (see introduction)

1 tablespoon soaked dried fruits of your choice (I like to use raisins or golden sultanas)
mixed seeds, to serve

Serves 1

Mix the cold cooked pearl barley with the yogurt and top with soaked almonds and dried fruits.

Note: The night before you want to eat, cook the pearl barley in a large saucepan of water, following the packet instructions. I simmer mine for about 25 minutes and then test for texture. The barley should have tripled in volume and will be tender but still a bit chewy when done. Drain well. Let cool and refrigerate overnight. The remaining pearl barley will keep in the fridge for several days, ready for a quick, healthy breakfast.

Freya's Blueberry Porridge

In Scandinavia, we don't have blueberries in our forests – we have bilberries. Although in Sweden these are called 'blåbär', which literally translates as blueberries. Confused yet? Bilberries are blue all the way through, smaller and more juicy. They have higher levels of vitamins C and E and higher anthocyanins than cultivated blueberries. I've spent long summer days at my in-laws' place in Sweden walking, picking and eating bilberries. If you can get hold of them, they are great for this recipe, but I often use frozen blueberries.

100 g/generous 1 cup jumbo rolled oats (or use steel-cut oats if you want to reduce the cooking time a bit)
200 ml/generous ³⁄₄ cup unsweetened almond or normal milk
250–300 ml/1–1¹⁄₄ cups water
pinch of salt

100 g/³⁄₄ cup fresh or frozen bilberries or blueberries
agave syrup and sliced fresh fruit and extra berries (I've used strawberries and white currants), to serve (optional)

Serves 2

Put the oats and milk in a saucepan. Add 250 ml/1 cup of the water, the salt and three quarters of the berries. Bring to the boil, then cook on a low heat for around 10–15 minutes, stirring occasionally, until the berries and oats are cooked through. Squash the berries lightly with a fork to release the juice and your porridge will change colour to a deep purple. Add the rest of the water, if needed, so it is not too thick.

When cooked through, serve into bowls and top with fruit of your choice and the rest of the blueberries or bilberries, if you have them. I sometimes add a little agave syrup for extra sweetness if the berries are tart.

Cinnamon Bun French Toast

Imagine the situation – you have some leftover cinnamon buns.
It doesn't happen often, but it CAN happen. What does one do
with those useless, stale things? Cinnamon bun French toast
with vanilla syrup and cardamom yogurt, of course. The syrup
recipe makes an ample amount, but it will keep in the fridge for
a few weeks. If you can't be bothered, use maple syrup instead.

VANILLA SYRUP
150 g/³⁄₄ cup caster/
    superfine sugar
100 ml/¹⁄₃ cup plus
    1 tablespoon water
1 vanilla pod/bean
sea salt flakes (optional)

YOGURT TOPPING
200 g/1 cup thick Greek/
    plain Greek-style yogurt
ground cardamom,
to taste

FRENCH TOAST
3 eggs

pinch of salt
¹⁄₂ teaspoon ground cinnamon
50 g/generous ¹⁄₃ cup plain/
    all-purpose flour
small pinch of bicarbonate
    of soda/baking soda
125 ml/¹⁄₂ cup whole milk
4 cinnamon buns, sliced
    widthways in half (traditional
    Scandi yeast-based buns)
butter, for frying
fresh raspberries or
    blackberries, to serve

Serves 4

For the vanilla syrup, put the sugar and water in a saucepan, scrape the vanilla
pod/bean and add the pod and seeds to the pan. Boil gently for 4–5 minutes
on a medium-high heat, taking care not to burn the syrup. If it's reducing too
quickly, shorten the cooking time or your syrup will be too thick. Remove from
the heat and add salt flakes to taste, if you like (it intensifies the vanilla flavour).

For the yogurt topping, stir the cardamom into the yogurt, to taste – I like
freshly ground cardamom, but you can leave it plain if you are not a fan.

For the French toast, mix the eggs with the salt, cinnamon, flour and
bicarbonate of soda/baking soda. Pour in the milk, bit by bit, and stir into
a smooth batter. Place the bun pieces in a bowl and pour the batter over.
Mix to ensure all pieces are generously coated. Cover with clingfilm/plastic
wrap and leave for 10 minutes to soak through.

Heat some butter in a frying pan/skillet, then fry the pieces of bun until cooked
through and golden on both sides, adding more butter as needed. Arrange two
on each plate, top with cardamom yogurt and berries. Pour over syrup to taste.

Danish Breakfast Buns

On Sunday mornings in Denmark, someone will usually do the run to pick up bread from the bakers. We eat a lot of buns, commonly known as 'rundstykker' – literally meaning 'round pieces'. Most bakeries offer many different varieties. These with poppy seeds are my version of the most popular kind, but you can vary them as you like by adding different seeds or mixing in a different flour to vary the taste.

25 g/1 oz. fresh yeast or 13 g/
   2½ teaspoons active dried yeast
250 ml/1 cup plus 1 tablespoon
   lukewarm water (35–37°C/97–98°F)
100 ml/⅓ cup plus 1 tablespoon
   lukewarm whole milk
2 tablespoons caster/granulated sugar
1 teaspoon salt
approx. 450 g/3¼ cups white/strong
   bread flour (you might need a little
   more or less than this), plus extra
   for the work surface
2 tablespoons olive oil
beaten egg, to glaze
plenty of black poppy seeds,
   to decorate
butter, strong Scandi cheese and
   cloudberry/bakeapple jam/jelly, to
   serve (optional)

cooking thermometer

*2 baking sheets, lined with non-stick
   baking parchment*

Makes 12 buns

If using fresh yeast, put the lukewarm water, milk and sugar into the bowl of a stand mixer with the dough hook attached. Add the yeast and let dissolve. If using active dried yeast, follow the instructions on the packet – usually you whisk together the lukewarm liquid and yeast in a bowl and leave in a warm place for 15 minutes to activate and become frothy before using. Once activated, pour into the bowl of your stand mixer, then stir in the sugar until dissolved.

Note: If you want to prove these buns overnight, use cold liquids, let rise overnight in a cool place and bake first thing in the morning.

Mix the salt into the flour then add to the stand mixer. Add the oil and mix on a low speed for about 5 minutes, then turn the speed up to high and mix well for about 3 minutes more. The dough will be quite sticky – you can add a little more flour, if needed, to bring it together. Break off and stretch out a small piece of the dough. If it becomes translucent without breaking, then the gluten is well developed and your dough is ready. If not, knead for a little longer.

When ready, cover the bowl with clingfilm/plastic wrap and leave the dough to rise for at least an hour in a warm place until doubled in size. (If cold rising, leave overnight in a cool place.)

Dust your work surface with flour, then turn out the dough and knead through. Cut it into 12 equal pieces and roll each piece into neat round rolls. Space out evenly on the lined baking sheets. Cover with a damp kitchen cloth and leave to rise for another hour.

Preheat the oven to 180°C (350°F) Gas 4.

Brush each roll with beaten egg and sprinkle with plenty of poppy seeds. Place a tray containing 1 litre/4 cups of water in the bottom of your oven. The steam will help the buns to develop a proper crust. Bake the buns in the preheated oven for about 8–10 minutes until golden and baked through – you may need to turn the trays halfway through. Let cool a little before eating with butter, strong Scandi cheese and a dollop of cloudberry/bakeapple jam/jelly.

open sandwiches

The Danish national dish is arguably
the humble open sandwich, although they
are big in both Sweden and Norway, too.
In every town in Denmark you can find
restaurants and speciality shops serving
open sandwiches that look like little works
of art. When making them at home, use
good quality ingredients (as everything
will be on show), and do try to get a well-
balanced topping by incorporating protein,
crunch, fresh notes and creamy indulgent
flavours. Here, I've included a mixture
of some traditional and less traditional
recipes. Two per person makes for a good
lunch, but you could also create smaller
ones as canapés or lighter bites.

Rare Steak Open Sandwiches

In Denmark, thinly sliced roast beef is traditionally served on open sandwiches, but I love using thick slices of rare steak instead.

2 slices of dark rye bread, buttered
handful of lamb's lettuce/corn salad
200 g/7 oz. rare steak in the cut of your choice (cold or just rested), cut into thick slices
4 slices pickled cucumber
2 large tablespoons Remoulade Sauce (see page 112 or store-bought)
grated fresh horseradish or horseradish sauce
Crispy Onion Rings (see below or store-bought)
freshly chopped parsley, to garnish

CRISPY ONION RINGS
1 tablespoon plain/all-purpose flour
2 small onions, sliced into rings
125 ml/½ cup vegetable oil, for frying
salt and freshly ground black pepper

cooking thermometer

Makes 2 open sandwiches

To make the crispy onion rings, put the flour in a plastic sandwich bag and season with salt and pepper. Add the onions and shake until coated. Discard excess flour.

Fill a small saucepan one third of the way up with vegetable oil. Heat the oil to 130–140°C (265–285°F). If the oil is too hot, your onions will burn, and if it is too cold they will be soggy, so take care with this.

Add a third of the onions to the hot oil and cook for a few minutes or until golden brown. Remove with a slotted spoon and drain on paper towels. Repeat the frying process twice more with the rest of the onions.

Top both slices of the buttered rye bread with your salad leaves. Arrange the slices of steak on the bread, then add pickled cucumber slices and a dollop of remoulade sauce to each. Add the horseradish and pile on the crispy onions. Season with salt and pepper and garnish with chopped parsley to finish.

Chicken Open Sandwiches

This works just as well in a two-slice sandwich as it does on an open sandwich, but I just love serving this chicken topping in our café with the beautiful sprouted fennel seeds on top.

2 slices of sourdough or seeded crusty bread
a little cream cheese or butter, for spreading
4–6 slices cucumber, shaved very thinly lengthways on a mandoline
sprouted fennel seeds, to serve

CHICKEN MIXTURE
200 g/7 oz. cooked chicken (I favour thigh or leg meat), shredded or cut into pieces
handful of petit pois peas, podded, then blanched
small ¼ bulb thinly sliced fennel
80 ml/⅓ cup crème fraîche
1 tablespoon mayonnaise
1 spring onion/scallion, sliced
1 tablespoon freshly chopped mint
1 teaspoon freshly chopped flat-leaf parsley
½ teaspoon Dijon mustard
dash of vinegar
freshly squeezed lemon juice, to taste
salt and freshly ground black pepper

Makes 2 open sandwiches

Mix the ingredients for the chicken topping together and season to taste with salt and pepper.

Lightly toast your slices of bread and spread both with a little cream cheese or butter. Arrange the slices of cucumber on top. Spoon the chicken mixture over and scatter with the sprouted fennel seeds to serve.

Gravadlax Open Sandwiches

This classic cured salmon recipe makes more than needed for two sandwiches, but leftovers will keep nicely for 3–5 days in the fridge.

2 slices of dark rye
    bread, buttered
handful of lamb's
    lettuce/corn salad
100–120 g/3½–4½ oz.
    Gravadlax (see below)
4–6 slices thinly shaved
    cucumber
handful of dill sprigs
handful of pea shoots
4 tablespoons Mustard
    Dressing (see right)
freshly ground black
    pepper

GRAVADLAX
500 g/18 oz. good-quality
    fresh salmon fillet,
    skin-on (the middle bit
    if taking from a side)
30 g/1 oz. salt
40 g/3¼ tablespoons
    white sugar

1 generous teaspoon
    white peppercorns,
    crushed
1 tablespoon gin, vodka
    or aquavit (optional)
1 large bunch fresh dill

MUSTARD DRESSING
2 tablespoons Swedish
    mustard (such as
    Slotts Senap, or go for
    a good grainy Dijon)
4 tablespoons finely
    chopped fresh dill
1 tablespoon white wine
    vinegar
1 teaspoon white sugar
salt and freshly ground
    black pepper
100 ml/⅓ cup cold
    pressed rapeseed or
    good olive oil

Makes 2 open sandwiches

Freeze the salmon below -18°C (-4°F) for 48 hours before you plan to make the gravadlax. Defrost in the fridge, then remove any bones with clean tweezers.

Cut the salmon widthways down the middle into two. Mix together the salt, sugar and white pepper. Dab the alcohol mixed with a little water on both pieces of salmon, then rub the salt and sugar mix into the flesh.

Chop the dill and place on top of one flesh-side of salmon, then place the other flesh-side down on top and wrap tightly together with clingfilm/plastic wrap, ensuring the two flesh sides meet. Place in a plastic bag

in the fridge and turn over 2–3 times a day for 2–3 days to ensure the fish is evenly cured. The salmon is ready when the colour changes to become slightly translucent.

Mix together all the ingredients for the mustard dressing, apart from the oil, in a bowl. Whisk in the oil slowly, starting with a few drops and then adding in a thin stream until you have a good creamy consistency.

When ready to serve, discard the dill and thinly slice the salmon, flesh side-up and diagonally, discarding the skin. Pile salad leaves and salmon slices on top of the buttered bread. Finish with cucumber slices, dill sprigs, pea shoots, the mustard dressing and black pepper.

Simple Salmon Open Sandwiches

This is a great light recipe for summer, when you don't want to spend too long in a warm kitchen.

2 hard-boiled eggs,
    chopped
2 tablespoons good
    quality mayonnaise
3–4 heaped tablespoons
    cress
2 tablespoons chopped
    capers
handful of salad leaves
    such as rocket/arugula

2 slices of dark rye
    seeded bread, buttered
150 g/5½ oz. cooked
    salmon fillet, flaked
squeeze of lemon juice
freshly chopped chives,
    to garnish

Makes 2 open sandwiches

Mix the chopped egg with salt and pepper and the mayonnaise. Combine with half the cress and half of the capers.

Arrange the salad leaves on the base of the bread. Add the egg mixture to one side and the flaked salmon pieces to the other side. Finish with a squeeze of lemon juice and then garnish with the remaining cress, capers and chopped chives.

Avocado & Egg Open Sandwiches

These pretty open sandwiches work for both breakfast and lunch.

2 slices of dark rye bread, buttered

4–6 slices cucumber, shaved very thinly lengthways on a mandoline

1 large firm, but ripe, avocado (if too mushy you end up with smashed avo)

2 not quite hard-boiled eggs, cold and finely sliced in an egg slicer

1 spring onion/scallion, sliced

handful of sprouted beetroot seeds or alfalfa

handful of chia seeds or seeds of your choice

pea shoots, to garnish

salt and freshly ground black pepper

HERB MAYONNAISE

mayonnaise mixed with very finely chopped fresh herbs of your choice such as parsley, chives, basil or dill

Makes 2 open sandwiches

Arrange the cucumber slices to cover the base of the buttered bread.

Split the avocado in half and remove the stone/pit. Use a spoon to carefully scoop out each half of flesh from its skin in one go, leaving each as intact as possible.

Place each half on a chopping board, flat-side down. Use a sharp knife to make cuts widthways at 5-mm/¹/₄-inch intervals all the way through. Gently use your hand to push the slices to the side so that they fan out.

Use a spatula to lift and place one fanned avocado half each on one slice of buttered bread. On top of these, add one sliced egg each. Add a dollop of the herb mayonnaise, then scatter both sandwiches with the spring onion/scallion, beetroot seeds, chia seeds and pea shoots. Season well with salt and freshly ground black pepper to serve.

Skagenröra Open Sandwiches

One of the most famous appetizers in Scandinavia is undoubtedly the 'Toast Skagen' – fried bread topped with prawns/shrimp in mayonnaise and plenty of fresh herbs. You can also serve this topping as part of a smörgåsbord with crispbread or toasted white bread. Try to use really good quality prawns/shrimp – ones in brine are what I use if we don't have fresh prawns handy. They keep their flavour well and are widely available.

4 slices of dark rye bread, buttered

2 handfuls of mixed salad leaves

2 handfuls of sprouted beetroot seeds

SKAGENRÖRA

100 ml/¹/₃ cup crème fraîche

50 ml/¹/₄ cup mayonnaise

3 tablespoons finely chopped fresh dill, plus extra to garnish

3 tablespoons finely chopped fresh chives

1 shallot, finely chopped

¹/₂ teaspoon grated

lemon zest

¹/₂ teaspoon Dijon mustard

¹/₂ teaspoon grated fresh horseradish or horseradish sauce

freshly squeezed lemon juice, to taste

300 g/10¹/₂ oz. good quality prawns/shrimp or a mixture of prawns/crayfish tails

salt and freshly ground black pepper

Makes 4 open sandwiches (with leftover skagenröra)

Mix all the ingredients for the skagenröra in a bowl, adding the prawns/shrimp or crayfish tails at the end. Season to taste with salt and pepper and then refrigerate for an hour to allow the flavours to mingle.

Top the bread with salad leaves and a generous portion of skagenröra, then scatter with sprouted beetroot seeds. Garnish with dill to serve.

Scandinavian Easter

When I think back to Easter at home as a child, I always see our garden with patches of the last, sad, half-melted blobs of snow on the grass, broken by bright snowdrops and yellow winter aconite flowers.

As I'm from the flat south of Denmark, Easter was always about those first few rays of sunshine and daylight breaking through, marking the end of a long winter. No more snow, no more cold. Family get-togethers for long Easter lunches, running around in the forest collecting twigs for decorations or hunting for eggs. Every home has budding twigs displayed in vases, usually filled with little hollow egg shells, painted in different patterns and colours. In Sweden, people also hang coloured feathers in their Easter decorations.

For many Scandinavians, Easter is the first sign of spring stirring in the frozen ground below. After months of seemingly endless darkness and ice, we start to wake from our hibernation and spring into action. When the daylight once again hits our senses, we naturally want to spend more time outside, as much as we can really, and every opportunity to do so is relished. Easter is peak hiking time, even if it's still quite cold in many areas. It is also the last chance for skiing for a lot of people as we head to our cottages in the northern mountains of

Once in a while, when Easter comes late, the trees are starting to go green and we may even dare to leave our winter coats at home.

Norway and Sweden to catch a last few runs on the slopes. In Denmark, where there are no mountains at all, people head to their beach cottages and hope for the first chance of sun and warmth to sit outside (even just for a few hours). The weather is still unpredictable, but once in a while, when Easter comes late, the trees are starting to go green and we may even dare to leave our winter coats at home.

Traditions during Easter vary across Scandinavia. In Denmark, kids write 'gækkebreve' – letters on cut-out paper to send to friends and family. These secret messages contain an Easter rhyme, but the sender keeps their identity hidden by replacing their name with dots. If the recipient guesses who the letter-writer is, then an Easter egg must be given to the receiver by the sender, or vice versa if not. Most grandparents are particularly rubbish at guessing, funnily enough.

In Sweden, kids dress up as little Easter witches – a tradition dating back to pagan times – and go from door-to-door singing and asking for sweets or coins

in a Swedish version of trick-or-treating. These little witches are called 'påskkärringar' (literally 'Easter witches') – and they wear headscarves and long dresses, with red painted cheeks and freckles. Across Sweden, Easter witches feature heavily everywhere in the decorations, but you don't see them in the other Scandinavian countries (although Danes do have similar Midsummer witches instead a few months later).

In Norway, where every holiday is centred around the 'hytte' cottage and about getting as far away from any towns and cities as possible, people head north. There, Easter is all about catching the last few weeks of snow in the mountains. Cities in Norway during Easter are eerily quiet, as everyone rushes to their cottages for those last few ski runs and to get a slight tan from the strong sun in the mountains.

The whole Easter holiday is about celebrating the coming of spring, looking forward to the months of warmth ahead and waving goodbye to the long winter. It is a massive boost of positive energy for all.

Cottage Cheese, Cucumber & Radish Open Sandwiches

In Denmark, this recipe is often made with rygeost – a young cheese which is smoked over hay and nettles. My grandfather was a master at making rygeost and I remember helping out in my grandparents' smokery as a child. You can't get rygeost outside Denmark, so I often make this with cottage cheese instead. It's a great, fresh and simple open sandwich option.

2 slices of dark rye bread, buttered
1 x 10-cm/4-inch piece of cucumber, halved, deseeded and shaved very thinly lengthways on a mandoline
6 large radishes (or a few more if using smaller)
1 x 200-g/7-oz. tub cottage cheese
2 tablespoons freshly snipped chives, plus extra to garnish
freshly squeezed lemon juice, to taste
salt and freshly ground black pepper
handful of watercress or Indian cress, to garnish

Makes 2 open sandwiches

Arrange the ribbons of sliced cucumber on the rye bread, folded back on themselves once. This layer of cucumber will protect the bread from getting soggy too quickly from the cottage cheese, so try to make it cover the bread evenly.

Chop three quarters of the radishes into small pieces and finely slice the rest into thin rounds. Put the cottage cheese in a bowl and add the chopped radishes and chives. Add lemon juice and salt and pepper to taste and mix well.

Split the cottage cheese mixture between the two slices of bread and garnish with the finely sliced rounds of radish, chives and the cress. Serve with plenty of extra freshly ground black pepper.

Beetroot, Egg & Pumpkin Seed Open Sandwiches

You don't always need meat or fish to make a really satisfying open sandwich. The vegetarian topping combinations can be just as exciting and diverse. This one is one of my favourites, the beetroot/beet and egg are so delicious together.

2 slices of dark rye bread, buttered
150 g/5½ oz. Beetroot Salad (see page 65)
2 not quite hard-boiled eggs, quartered
2 teaspoons capers, finely chopped (optional)
alfalfa or beetroot/ beet sprouts
2 tablespoons toasted and chopped walnuts
pumpkin seeds, to garnish
salt and freshly ground black pepper

Makes 2 open sandwiches

Divide the beetroot/beet salad across the base of the two slices of buttered bread.

Arrange the eggs on top (one egg per slice). Scatter over the capers (if using), alfalfa sprouts and walnuts. Garnish with pumpkin seeds. Season well with plenty of salt and freshly ground black pepper.

Fish Cake Open Sandwiches with Tartar Dressing

'Fiskekaker' are a dinner staple in Norway and Denmark. This recipe makes 6–8 fish cakes but you can serve them for dinner and use the leftovers for these sandwiches.

2 slices of rye bread, buttered
pea shoots, to garnish
wedges of lemon, to serve

FISH CAKES
300 g/10½ oz. skinless
  boneless cod fillets
½ teaspoon salt
1 egg
2 tablespoons freshly
  chopped dill
1 shallot, chopped
½ carrot, finely grated
1 tablespoon plain/
  all-purpose flour
dash of single/light cream
freshly grated nutmeg
squeeze of lemon juice
salt and black pepper
butter and olive oil, for frying

TARTAR DRESSING
100 g/½ cup good quality
  mayonnaise
3 tablespoons chopped
  gherkins
1 tablespoon capers, chopped
1 small shallot, finely
  chopped
½ teaspoon Dijon mustard
2 tablespoons freshly
  chopped parsley
2 teaspoon freshly chopped
  chives
squeeze of lemon juice
flaked sea salt and freshly
  ground black pepper

*Makes 2 open sandwiches
(8–10 fish cakes)*

To make the tartar dressing, mix together all the ingredients in a small bowl and leave in the fridge for the flavours to mingle.

Meanwhile, put the fish in a food processor with the salt and blitz briefly until chopped through. Add the rest of the fish cake ingredients and blitz again until you have a smooth mixture.

Heat up a good knob/pat of butter with a glug of oil in a frying pan/skillet. Form large egg-sized fish cakes using a spoon and the palm of your hand. Place in the pan and fry the fish cakes for about 3–4 minutes on each side until cooked through. You may need to do this in batches.

Cut the cooked fish cakes in half and arrange three halves on each slice of buttered rye bread. Top with tartar dressing. Serve warm or cold garnished with pea shoots and a wedge of lemon on the side for squeezing over.

Hot-smoked Trout Open Sandwiches with Dill & Apple

Summer anywhere in Scandinavia means lots of salmon and trout – any way, any kind. I love smoked trout. It goes well with any type of crusty bread or toast, and fresh flavours such as tart apple and cucumber. Not forgetting some fresh dill to lift it, too.

2 pieces of toasted seeded sourdough or crispbread
a little cream cheese, for spreading
salad leaves, such as rocket/arugula
130 g/4½ oz. (approx. 2 pieces) hot-smoked trout fillets

DILL & APPLE SALAD
½ green apple, finely sliced on a mandoline
¼ cucumber, deseeded and finely sliced on a mandoline
3 tablespoons white wine vinegar
½ teaspoon white sugar
2 tablespoons finely chopped fresh dill, plus extra to garnish
salt and freshly ground black pepper

Makes 2
open sandwiches

Put the sliced apple and cucumber in a small bowl. Mix the vinegar with the sugar in another bowl until dissolved. Season the vinegar to taste with salt and black pepper, then add the dill and pour over the apple and cucumber. Mix together and leave to sit until ready to use.

Place the toasted sourdough or crispbread on a serving plate and spread with a bit of cream cheese. Add the salad leaves and fish fillets on top with the apple and cucumber salad. Garnish with dill and extra black pepper. Serve immediately, or the bread will go soggy.

salads & sharing plates

People often think that hygge is just for the winter, but this is not the case. Hygge at its core is about spending time with the people you like, being able to relax and savour the moment while you are in it. Summer is the perfect time to spend time with loved ones and create happy memories. Lots of hygge is to do with food – a big picnic rug or a big table full of delicious food and good friends for company. What could be better? The simple pleasures of good food and warm weather tend to make people very happy – they are a perfect recipe for summer hygge.

Smoked Mackerel Rillettes with Rye Crisps

This is a super-easy way to prepare an appetizer or light lunch. Rillettes are a coarse, potted meat similar to pâté that are stirred together and spread on toast. They're usually made with fatty pork (or duck) leftovers, but I love making rillettes with fish. This recipe works well with both smoked mackerel and smoked salmon.

8–12 thin slices of rye bread
  or store-bought rye crisps
  (available in supermarkets)
200 ml/³⁄₄ cup crème fraîche
2 teaspoons Dijon mustard
3 tablespoons chopped chives
squeeze of fresh lime juice
¹⁄₂ teaspoon horseradish sauce
  (optional)
300 g/10¹⁄₂ oz. smoked mackerel
freshly ground black pepper
  (hold the salt until you taste it,
  some mackerel is very salty)

TO SERVE
¹⁄₄ small fennel bulb
¹⁄₂ apple
freshly squeezed lemon juice
fresh pea shoots

4 individual serving glasses

*Serves 4 as a generous
appetizer or light lunch*

If using rye bread, preheat the oven to 140°C (275°F) Gas 1. Slice the rye bread very thinly and place on a baking tray. If the bread is too thick it will be hard to eat as crispy bread, so do make sure it is thinly sliced. Bake in the preheated oven for about 10–20 minutes (depending on your bread) until completely dry. You can make it several days ahead and store in an airtight container.

Mix the crème fraîche with the mustard, chives, lime juice and horseradish (if using). Remove the skin from the mackerel and add the fish to the crème fraîche mixture. Stir just until mixed – I like my rillettes with a few chunky bits, but some people prefer it smoother. If you like yours smoother, simply mix a while longer. Check for seasoning and add black pepper to taste. Spoon the mixture into the serving glasses. Chill until ready to serve.

When ready to serve, slice the fennel and apple very thinly, ideally using a mandoline. Add a squeeze of lemon juice to stop the apple going brown and mix well. Serve the apple and fennel salad with pea shoots, the glasses of mackerel and the rye toast on the side. You may need extra toast as the mackerel makes a generous portion.

Raw Courgette Salad with Västerbotten Cheese

Eating courgettes/zucchini raw is not that traditional, but at the café we love using it uncooked in different types of salads. This salad, in particular, looks so pretty on the plate. If you don't have a mandoline slicer, use a peeler, but try to peel whole thin slices lengthways, as it looks better on the plate. You can also use a cheese plane instead if you have one. We use Västerbotten cheese at the café, but you can also substitute with pecorino or any similar aged cheese. It's the saltiness of the cheese that really lifts the raw courgette/zucchini – and with the dressing as well as the nuts, it makes for a really lovely side dish.

50 g/⅔ cup flaked/slivered almonds
2 medium-sized courgettes/zucchini
1 small bunch of rocket/arugula
　　(or other strong-flavoured salad
　　leaves of your choice)
50 g/2 oz. Västerbotten cheese,
　　shaved (or use a good pecorino
　　instead)

DRESSING
3 tablespoons olive oil
1 tablespoon freshly squeezed
　　lemon juice
1 tablespoon white wine vinegar
¼ teaspoon Dijon mustard
1 teaspoon sugar
salt and freshly ground black pepper

Serves 2–3

Lightly toast the almonds over a gentle heat in a dry frying pan/skillet and set aside.

Shave the courgettes/zucchini into thin strips lengthways. You can use a mandoline for this, or a flat metal cheese plane also works well. You want long, thin flat strips.

Place the courgette/zucchini strips in a big bowl, then add the leaves and mix gently. Add the cheese and fold in.

Combine the dressing ingredients in a small bowl, whisk well and season to taste. This salad doesn't need much dressing, so don't pour it all on at once – taste as you go along.

Scatter the toasted almonds on top of the salad and serve at once.

Black Rice & Salmon Salad

Black rice lends itself well to being used cold in salads. It is known sometimes
as 'forbidden rice', and sometimes as 'black venus rice'. It has a hard husk
and a great bite to it – and, of course, a wonderful dark colour.

200 g/generous 1 cup
   uncooked black rice

1 cucumber

1 green apple

1 shallot, finely chopped

squeeze of lemon juice

1 bunch of fresh dill, chopped

2 tablespoons freshly chopped
   parsley

1 tablespoon freshly chopped mint
   (optional)

150 g/5½ oz. hot-smoked salmon

DRESSING

2 tablespoons white wine vinegar

4 tablespoons good quality olive
   or rapeseed oil

1 tablespoon honey

1 tablespoon freshly squeezed
   lemon or lime juice (plus
   extra as needed)

salt and freshly ground black
   pepper

*Serves 4 individual portions
or 6–7 as a side dish*

Rinse the black rice a few times, then bring to the boil in a large
pan of water. Cook until al dente following the packet instructions.
(It can take about 30 minutes to cook, it takes a while, a bit like brown
rice). Once cooked, rinse well to remove the excess colour. Set aside
for a moment and leave to cool.

Slice the cucumber lengthways, then scrape out the seeds and
chop into ½ cm/¼ inch pieces. Chop the apple into similarly sized
small pieces. Add the cucumber, apple and shallot to a serving bowl
with a squeeze of lemon juice to keep the apple fresh. Add the cooked
and cooled black rice, dill, parsley and mint (if using). Flake in the
salmon pieces and mix gently to combine everything together.

Whisk together the dressing ingredients in a small bowl and season
to taste. Pour the dressing over the salad and stir. Do adjust the
seasoning once you have done this – it may need more lemon juice
or even a squeeze of lime (this depends on the saltiness of the fish
and the sweetness of the apple you have used).

My Summer Slaw

I love coleslaw, I really do, but I detest the gloopy factory-made rubbish that seems to have become standard fare in supermarkets all over. If you ask me, the secret to a good slaw is lightly pickling the cabbage base before adding a punchy, flavourful dressing.

CABBAGE BASE

300 g/5 cups shredded white
   and red cabbage

1 red onion

2 large (or 3 smaller) carrots

100 ml/⅓ cup plus 1 tablespoon water

100 ml/generous ⅓ cup plus
   1 tablespoon white wine vinegar

3 generous tablespoons icing/
   confectioners' sugar

½ teaspoon salt

DRESSING

3 generous tablespoons good quality
   mayonnaise

3 tablespoons buttermilk

1 tablespoon icing/confectioners'
   sugar

1 teaspoon Dijon mustard

1 teaspoon white wine vinegar (only
   if needed)

½ teaspoon celery salt

1 teaspoon grated fresh horseradish
   or horseradish sauce

salt and freshly ground black pepper

TO SERVE

3 spring onions/scallions, sliced

50 g/generous ½ cup toasted,
   chopped walnuts

30–35 g/¼ cup pumpkin seeds

Serves 4–6 as a side dish

Place the shredded white and red cabbage in a large bowl. Finely slice the red onion into half rounds, and then grate (or julienne, if you can be bothered) the carrots and add both to the bowl.

In another bowl or jug/pitcher, mix together the water, white wine vinegar, icing/confectioners' sugar and salt. Pour over the cabbage, then cover the bowl and shake well. Leave for at least one hour, ideally two – shake it once in a while.

Press the cabbage free of excess vinegar liquid and leave in a sieve/strainer until excess vinegar has drained. The cabbage will now be softer and the onion appear almost a little cooked. Make sure the vinegar is well pressed out or the end result will be too acidic.

Mix together the ingredients for the dressing. Mix the dressing with the slaw and taste – it should be a bit tangy. If not, add a teaspoon extra of vinegar (this depends how much of the pickle juice was pressed out – it is easier to add a bit than remove if too much).

Just before serving, fold in the spring onion/scallions and toasted chopped walnuts. Sprinkle over the pumpkin seeds for extra crunch. This coleslaw is extra delicious on days two and three – when it will be pink (if you have used red cabbage).

Curried Cauliflower & Rye Grain Salad

This salad is so delicious and a perfect way to use the humble cauliflower. Our good friend Kobi Ruzicka came up with this a few years back. We didn't put it on the café menu for a while and then, one day, we found his notes and, well, it was a bit like discovering your favourite toy that you thought you'd lost. Kobi left London and now runs his own restaurant in Hobart – you should look him up if you ever go to Tasmania. In fact, it's worth a detour to visit. Even if the detour is from, say, the UK. Use whatever grain you like, at the café, we use boiled whole rye grain. Cooked spelt or pearl barley also work well – anything with a good, firm bite.

1 medium head of cauliflower
glug of olive oil
1–2 teaspoon(s) mild curry powder, to taste
½ bunch fresh flat-leaf parsley, roughly chopped
1 bunch spring onions/scallions
75 g/2½ oz. feta cheese
a good handful of plump raisins
100–150 g/5½ oz. cooked grains such as rye grain, pearl barley or spelt (see Note)
squeeze of fresh lemon juice
glug of good rapeseed or olive oil
salt and freshly ground black pepper

Serves 4 as a side dish

Preheat the oven to 160°C (325°F) Gas 3.

Cut the cauliflower into bite-sized florets. Put the florets in a bowl and toss together with the olive oil, curry powder and salt and pepper to taste. Spread out on a baking tray and roast in the preheated oven for about 10 minutes – the cauliflower should be more on the firm side than soft.

Meanwhile, place the parsley in a large salad serving bowl. Remove the outer layer from the spring onions/scallions and finely slice both the green and white bits at an angle and add to the bowl. Lightly crumble the feta into the same bowl with your fingers and set aside.

When the cauliflower is cooked, remove from the oven and allow to cool slightly. Add to the bowl along with the raisins and cooked grains. Stir, then add oil and a squeeze of lemon juice, if needed, then season to taste with salt and pepper and serve. It is delicious when eaten slightly warm, but also nice cold the next day too.

Note: If cooking rye grains from scratch, ideally soak them overnight before use – then they take 20 minutes to cook to al dente. If you don't have time to soak them, then simply double the cooking time. Pearl barley and spelt take about 30-35 minutes to cook.

Lighter Beetroot Salad

This super-traditional pickled beetroot/beet salad can be found in most smörgåsbords across the Nordic countries. You can eat it with cold meatballs or salmon, on sandwiches or just as a side dish with your main meal. In this version I have used skyr (an Icelandic cultured dairy product with the texture of yogurt) instead of mayonnaise to keep it a bit lighter. Skyr is naturally low in fat but high in protein, and because it is thick set, it really holds salads like this together without adding too much fat to the equation. If you would prefer the original version, simply replace the skyr with as much mayo as you need to produce a creamy pink salad. The colour will develop overnight to become darker.

300 g/10½ oz. pickled
   beetroot/beet from
   a jar, drained
1 tart apple (such as a
   Granny Smith)
200 ml/scant 1 cup skyr
   or plain quark
50 g/⅓ cup pickled
   cucumbers, chopped

dash of balsamic vinegar
squeeze of fresh lemon
   juice
2 tablespoons freshly
   chopped chives
salt and freshly ground
   black pepper

Serves 2 as a side

Drain the pickled beetroot/beet and chop into bite-sized pieces. Peel and chop the apple into similar-sized small pieces.

Combine the apple and beetroot/beet in a serving bowl, then add the other ingredients and mix, seasoning to taste with salt and pepper at the end.

Note: Certain types of pickled beetroot/beets use sweeteners and will need more sourness to balance them out. Others are too sour and may need a little icing/confectioners' sugar. Season to taste at the end.

Asparagus & Bean Salad

A simple but delicious salad that makes the best of asparagus and broad/fava bean season. Västerbotten is an aged Swedish cheese, but you can use pecorino or Grana Padano instead. This is a nice salad to have with a smörgåsbord or BBQ.

200 g/7 oz. broad/fava
   beans in pods (or
   150 g/5½ oz. if buying
   ready-podded)
1 bunch of asparagus
   (approx. 200 g/7 oz.)
handful of fresh tarragon
   leaves, chopped
50 g/2 oz. shavings of
   Västerbotten cheese
handful of toasted
   pinenuts or hazelnuts
   (optional)

DRESSING
3 tablespoons good
   cold-pressed olive
   or rapeseed oil
1 tablespoon balsamic
   vinegar
1 tablespoon lemon juice
1 teaspoon honey
salt and freshly ground
   black pepper

Serves 2 as a side

Whisk together the dressing ingredients and set aside.

Pod the broad/fava beans from the outer large pods, then cook them in a large saucepan of boiling water for 1 minute. Throw in the asparagus and cook for a further 2 minutes (if the asparagus spears are quite large, then put them in at the start of cooking). Plunge all the vegetables into a bowl of ice-cold water to stop the cooking process.

Set the beans to one side and then remove the whitish outer pod (second podding) to reveal the green tender bean inside. Yes, this takes a little time and if you can't be bothered, I'm sure the bean police won't be out to get you.

Slice the asparagus spears in half lengthways, then place in your salad serving bowl and fold in the beans. Add the tarragon and shavings of cheese to taste, then pour over the dressing. For a nutty finish, top with toasted pinenuts or hazelnuts. Serve immediately.

Midsummer smörgåsbord

Midsummer is celebrated by all Scandinavians. There are different traditions,
but the meaning is the same: to honour the longest days of the year, revel
in the never-ending light, and praise nature.

When June comes around, we Scandinavians start
to get excited. The kids prepare for their summer
holidays (June through to early August) and everything
is so bright and full of life. Our seasons are a little later
than other northern European countries, so this is when
the local strawberries reach us and we start to indulge
in all the beautiful gifts from Mother Nature's summer
pantry. Every year, the first taste of strawberries, picked
in the garden on a late June day, takes me right back
home to my grandmother's garden. It is a sign that
summer has really begun – time to enjoy it while it lasts.

In Denmark and Norway, midsummer is known as
'sankthansaften' (St John's Eve) and is always celebrated
on 23rd June by lighting bonfires by the seashore or in
town centres. The Danes like to throw effigies of witches
on the flames – the belief is that by burning them
on the stake, you help send them to the German
mountains to dance with the Devil. The long
midsummer evening is spent on the beach, watching
the bonfires burn. It is a pretty spectacular evening to fly
in over Denmark as you can see the bonfires outlining
the country all along the coast. Families will gather with

neighbours and friends, maybe grill a few sausages on the hot embers of the bonfire and then have a swim in the clear waters of the light evening.

In Sweden, midsummer is celebrated on the nearest Friday. It's a public holiday and everybody celebrates – it's a day best spent surrounded by nature, and cities are left deserted as people flock to their cottages. Flower garlands are made in the meadows, and the saying goes that if a young woman picks seven different wild flowers on midsummer's eve and puts them under her pillow, she will dream of the person she will marry.

Midsummer celebrations are centred around food and the big smörgåsbord feast served at home or brought along in a picnic. Here, new potatoes with dill always feature (see page 77), as does tangy matjes herring, or, any pickled herring (see page 74). Added to this are classic dishes such as Beetroot Salad (see page 65), Swedish meatballs, Västerbotten Paj (see page 93) and

an array of lovely summer salads and sliced meats. All of this is enjoyed with a helping of Scandinavian aquavit (see page 171), a strong, grain-based spirit. Each shot must be downed in one and accompanied by a good sing-song of the famous 'Helan går' tune. After a few of these, most non-Swedish people's language skills improve and everybody can join in. After a while, it's time to dance around the flower-decorated midsummer pole. People hold hands and jump around, singing traditional songs and generally laughing a lot. Some fall over. Everybody joins in, old and young, to celebrate the never-ending daylight of midsummer.

Experiencing midsummer in Scandinavia is truly magical, and the lasting light really is something quite special. If you can't make it up to the Northern shores, most big cities around the world have Scandinavian immigrant and populations, and there is bound to be a midsummer picnic or event happening. Just take it easy on that aquavit.

Pea Purée Dip

This herb-packed dip works particularly well as a base for open sandwiches with smoked oily fish.

500 g/3¾ cups frozen peas
pinch of baking soda/ bicarbonate of soda
½ bunch fresh chives
⅓ bunch fresh tarragon (2–3 sprigs)

good glug of olive oil
squeeze of fresh lemon juice, to taste
salt and freshly ground black pepper

Serves 4

Blanch the peas in boiling water with the baking soda/ bicarbonate of soda for 2–3 minutes (the baking soda helps the peas to keep their colour). Quickly plunge the peas into ice-cold water to stop the cooking process.

Add the peas to a food processor or use a stick blender to blitz until smooth. Adjust the seasoning to taste. If you like a creamier finish, add a dollop of Greek yogurt.

Beetroot Dip

This earthy dip is delicious served with simple crackers or flatbread. If you don't like the strong taste of cumin, you can replace it with fresh dill.

300 g/10½ oz. cooked beetroot/beets
50 g/⅓ cup toasted hazelnuts
1 tablespoon grated fresh horseradish or horseradish sauce
pinch of ground cumin

2 tablespoons Greek/ plain Greek-style yogurt
balsamic vinegar, to taste
squeeze of lemon juice
salt and freshly ground black pepper

Serves 4

Blend the beetroot/beets and toasted hazelnuts in a food processor or use a stick blender to blitz until smooth. Mix this smooth paste with the rest of the ingredients until well combined.

Nettle Dip

Fresh nettles taste a bit like spinach in my opinion, but they have a stronger aftertaste and are a bit coarser in texture. See the note below for more details on how to pick and treat raw nettles so that you don't sting yourself.

50 g/2 oz. nettle leaves (see Note)
1 shallot, chopped
¼ garlic clove, crushed
50 g/2 oz. Västerbotten or pecorino cheese, finely grated
1 spring onion/scallion, chopped
1 tablespoon mayonnaise

Greek/plain Greek-style yogurt, to taste
squeeze of fresh lemon juice, to taste
salt and freshly ground black pepper

Serves 4

First, wearing protective gloves, discard any thick stems and rough bits from the nettles. Rinse the leaves and then pop them into a saucepan of boiling water for around 2–3 minutes until soft. This will kill the stings.

Drain, then chop the nettle leaves. Add to a food processor or use a stick blender and blitz. Add the other dip ingredients (except the Greek yogurt and seasoning) and blitz again until fairly smooth.

Fold in the Greek yogurt and season to taste with salt and black pepper. Chill in the fridge for 30 minutes before serving.

Note: When foraging for nettles always wear protective gloves. Only use the new tips and leaves, not the old plants – the best season is April through to May in the UK where I live, but if you live elsewhere you can look this up online. Never pick nettles that have grown next to polluted roads.

Pickled Herring Two Ways

No smörgåsbord is complete without the infamous pickled herring. There are as many recipes for the sauces or dressings for herring as there are people who make them. Anything can be used – from vegetables to berries or creamier bases. If you are new to eating pickled herring, starting with one in a dressing is a good idea as you will get a good balance of flavours. Always serve dressed herring at the beginning of the meal along with a shot of chilled aquavit (see page 171).

Mustard Herring

This herring dressing is as traditional as they come. Every Nordic country has a favourite, in Sweden, the favourite is this mustard dressing.

150 g/5½ oz. (drained weight) plain pickled herring
2 tablespoons Swedish wholegrain mustard (or a grainy sweet mustard will work)
1 teaspoon Dijon mustard
1 tablespoon caster/granulated sugar
2 tablespoons white wine vinegar
2 tablespoons double/heavy cream

1 tablespoon crème fraîche
1 small shallot, finely chopped
100 ml/⅓ cup plus 1 tablespoon sunflower or other neutral oil
2 tablespoons finely chopped fresh dill
1 tablespoon chopped chives (optional)
salt and freshly ground black pepper

Serves 4

Drain the herring and discard the onion bits and brine.

In a bowl, mix everything together except the oil, herbs and herring. Slowly pour in the oil while whisking continuously so that the sauce emulsifies.

Stir in the herbs, then the herring. Leave the bowl in the fridge for a few hours to marinade, then serve with rye bread or crispbread.

Dill & Apple Herring

These flavours pair perfectly with slices of a good, strong Scandinavian hard cheese and crispbread or rye bread.

50 ml/¼ cup mayonnaise
100 ml/⅓ cup crème fraîche
1 teaspoon Dijon mustard
1 teaspoon honey
squeeze of fresh lemon juice, to taste
3 tablespoons finely chopped fresh chives
3 tablespoons freshly chopped dill
½ red apple, cut into small cubes

150 g/5½ oz. (drained weight) onion-pickled herring, cut into bite-sized pieces
salt and freshly ground black pepper
chopped red onion, to garnish
whole sprigs of dill, to garnish

Serves 4

In a bowl, mix together the mayonnaise, crème fraîche and mustard. Add the honey, salt, pepper and lemon juice and then fold in the chives and dill. Finally, add the apple and then the herring at the end.

Leave the bowl in the fridge for a few hours to let the flavours mingle. Garnish with chopped red onion.

Dill Pesto Potato Salad

Sometimes, normal pesto gets a bit boring! You may think that dill is too strong for a pesto like this, but it's not. It is super-easy to make and from one portion there will be leftovers to use in sandwiches (it goes well with chicken) – or you can even use it as a topping for salmon fillets before you pop them in the oven. Serve these potatoes as part of your summer BBQ.

500 g/18 oz. cooked skin-on new potatoes, cooled slightly

DILL PESTO
1 large bunch of fresh dill
1 tablespoon freshly chopped parsley
½ garlic clove
75 g/scant ⅔ cup walnuts
50 g/2 oz. grated Västerbotten cheese

(or another hard cheese with a deep flavour)
50–100 ml/¼–⅓ cup extra virgin or good quality olive oil
salt and freshly ground black pepper

Serves 4 as a side

In a food processor combine the dill, parsley, garlic and walnuts and pulse to roughly chop. Add three quarters of the grated cheese and 50 ml/¼ cup of the oil and pulse again until you have a finely chopped paste.

Remove from the food processor and add the rest of the cheese (if needed) and more oil until you have a pesto consistency (not too runny, but liquid enough that it can be used as a dressing). Taste and season with salt and black pepper.

Put the cooked potatoes and a few tablespoons of the pesto in a bowl. Mix until potatoes are well coated. You may need to add more pesto to taste.

Potato Salad with Skyr Dressing

I love skyr – it's naturally very low in fat and full of protein. It is a very old-fashioned dairy product that has been made in Iceland for over a thousand years, and in recent years, has gained popularity across the globe. It's served in a similar way to yogurt, and you can add toppings if you want to just eat it like that. It's cheap and filling without being too full of fat. Here's a creamy potato salad with skyr, in this recipe you can use plain quark if you can't find no-added-sugar plain skyr.

½ red onion, thinly sliced
3 tablespoons freshly chopped chives
a large handful of podded broad/fava beans (cooked and cold)
600–700 g/21–25 oz. cooked skin-on new potatoes, cold

SKYR DRESSING
250 g/1⅓ cups skyr or plain quark

1 tablespoon Dijon mustard
1 dollop of mayonnaise (optional – see Note)
1 tablespoon honey
1–2 tablespoon(s) apple cider vinegar, to taste
salt and freshly ground black pepper

Serves 4 as a side

Mix together the dressing ingredients and taste, adjusting the seasoning if necessary. Add the onion, chives and beans.

Cut the potatoes into bite-sized pieces and add to the dressing. Stir and serve.

Note: The addition of mayonnaise does add a hint of creaminess to this potato salad. If you are serving this with something quite light, you can probably afford to add the mayo – but if serving it with something fatty, I would usually leave it out.

Easy New Potato & Dill Salad

This makes a nice fresh bowl of potato salad, perfect for a summer buffet. The dressing is light and fresh, and if you want to make the salad even lighter, just add less of the dressing. It's truly one of those two-minute salads that takes some basic new potatoes to a different level.

1 kg/2¼ lb. of cooked skin-on new potatoes, warm or cool

MUSTARD DRESSING
75 ml/⅓ cup sunflower oil or other neutral oil
2 tablespoons white wine vinegar
1 tablespoon Dijon mustard
1 tablespoon caster/granulated sugar
1 shallot, very finely chopped
1 bunch of fresh dill, finely chopped
salt and freshly ground black pepper

Serves 4 as a side

You can use slightly warm potatoes or cooled ones straight out of the fridge for this dish, but only dress them just before serving for best results.

To make the dressing, whisk the oil, vinegar, mustard and sugar until the sugar has dissolved, then fold in the chopped shallot and dill. Season to taste with salt and pepper. Toss the dressing with the potatoes and ensure they are evenly covered.

Creamy Potato Salad

Just like my mother makes it. I love this with cold meatballs – a perfect al fresco lunch for summer.

500–600 g/18–21 oz. cooked skin-on new potatoes, cold and cut into bite-sized pieces

CREAMY DRESSING
75 g/⅓ cup Greek/plain Greek-style yogurt
75 g/⅓ cup mayonnaise
1 teaspoon Dijon mustard
4 spring onions/scallions, sliced
50 g/½ cup chopped pickled cucumber
6–7 radishes, sliced
sea salt and freshly ground black pepper

Serves 4 as a side

Mix everything together and leave in the fridge for a few hours for the flavours to mingle before serving. If you need more zing, add pickle juice or lemon juice.

Warm Summer Potatoes

This side goes well with summer fish dishes such as fried plaice (see page 112) or baked salmon.

knob/pat of butter
700 g/25 oz. cooked skin-on new potatoes, cold and cut in half
150 g/1 cup cooked peas (warm or cold is fine)
small bunch of freshly chopped dill
salt and freshly ground black pepper
handful of pea shoots

Serves 4 as a side

Melt the butter in a frying pan/skillet and fry off the potatoes for a few minutes until golden in places. Take off the heat, then add the peas and allow to warm through. Add the dill and season with salt and pepper (you might need to add a glug of olive oil if the potatoes feel a bit dry – some varieties are better with this than others). Stir through the pea shoots to serve.

Crispbread Pizza

A while ago, people in Sweden started making pizza out of crispbread. I always thought this was a wonderful idea. Pizza is amazing – no doubt about that – but we can't really justify eating it all the time. So, trust the Swedes to make it all very lagom and balanced by using a super-healthy base so that it's ready in five minutes! Leksands is my favourite brand of crispbread to use for this, because it is fairly thick and comes in big round slices, so it actually looks like pizza once it is cooked. However, you can use other brands and make smaller versions. I use both tomato purée and pesto as bases. Toppings will vary depending on your refrigerator's mood that day – but really, as long as they're gooey when melted and tasty, you're good to go.

a handful of fresh peas
5–6 asparagus spears
1 big round of crispbread (I use Leksands)
2 tablespoons green pesto, with a few drops of olive oil mixed in
ready-to-eat green tomatoes, sliced (if you can't find them, red are fine)
bocconcini or mozzarella balls, to taste
a good handful of grated cheese (I use a mixture of torn mozzarella and Cheddar)
salt and freshly ground black pepper

Makes 1 large crispbread pizza

Preheat the oven to 180°C (350°F) Gas 4.

Blanch the peas and asparagus in boiling water for 3 minutes and then plunge into ice-cold water to stop the cooking process.

Place the crispbread on a large baking sheet and lightly spread the base with pesto. Add the tomato, asparagus, peas and then the bocconcini or mozzarella, torn into small shreds if needed. Top with the grated cheese. Season with salt and pepper and bake in the preheated oven for around 5 minutes or until the cheese has melted.

Slice with a pizza cutter and serve immediately (it does not keep). If you want a meaty version, add some air-dried ham after cooking.

Danish Sausage Rolls

This is a must-have for picnics and lunchboxes across Denmark. Forget the flaky pastry and British-style sausages – we like ours with wiener-style sausages wrapped in yeasty bread dough. I use Swedish 'Prinskorv' or wiener sausages, but you can use any good quality hotdog sausages. Try not to use a mass-produced ketchup, as these tend to be full of additives and bake poorly. If you can't find a decent one, add a little tomato purée to thicken it up a bit. Ideally these should be eaten on the same day they are made, but if stored, they should be kept in the fridge, though this will make them go stale quicker. Freezing is a good option if by chance you actually have any leftover.

25 g/1 oz. fresh yeast or 13 g/
    2½ teaspoons active dried yeast
250 ml/1 cup plus 1 tablespoon
    lukewarm water (35–37°C/97–98°F)
1 tablespoon sugar
1 teaspoon salt
400–500 g/14–18 oz. white/strong
    bread flour
100 g/½ cup minus ½ tablespoons
    plain yogurt
50 ml/3½ tablespoons olive
    or rapeseed oil
½ egg (reserve the other half
    for brushing)
500 g/18 oz. (approx.) wiener sausages
    cut into sixteen 6–7 cm/2½-inch
    pieces
good quality tomato ketchup (see
    introduction)
white sesame seeds, to garnish

2 baking sheets, lined with non-stick
    baking parchment

Makes 16 sausage rolls

Put the fresh yeast and lukewarm water in the bowl of a stand mixer with a dough hook attached and mix until dissolved. If using active dried yeast, follow the instructions on the packet – usually whisk together the lukewarm liquid and yeast in a bowl and leave in a warm place for 15 minutes to activate and become frothy before using. Once activated, pour into the bowl of your stand mixer.

Add the sugar and stir again. Mix the salt into the flour and then, while mixing at a medium speed, start to add the flour – around half of it – and mix until well combined. Add the yogurt, oil and egg and keep mixing. Add more flour slowly, stopping when you have a mixture that starts to let go of the sides of the bowl. This will take around 5 minutes and you might not need all the flour.

Leave the dough to rise in a warm place, in a bowl covered with clingfilm/plastic wrap, for around 40 minutes or until doubled in size.

Roll the dough out on a lightly floured work surface, then split into two equal balls. Roll the first ball out into a circle of around 30 cm/11¾ inches in diameter, then use a pizza cutter to divide the dough into 8 triangles. Brush each triangle with ketchup (mostly at the wide section, leaving the tip clear), then place a sausage piece at the thick end and roll up, like a croissant, with the sausage at the centre. Place on the prepared baking sheets with end of the fold underneath. Repeat for the rest of the sausages and dough. Leave the dough to rise for a final 15–20 minutes, then brush with beaten egg and scatter with sesame seeds.

Preheat the oven to 180°C (350°F) Gas 4.

Bake the sausage rolls in the preheated oven for around 15 minutes or until the dough is baked through and the rolls are golden.

larger plates & mains

Memories of those wonderful evenings
when the sun doesn't set until almost
midnight and the weather is warm enough
to sit outside are one of the things that keep
us going through the cold winter months.
Summer is a time to meet up with friends
and families and share good, home-cooked
food. From the spring-time feasts of fish,
to elaborate summer barbecues and late-
summer crayfish parties, all our summer
food is designed to be enjoyed outside in the
open air – as much as the ever-changing
Scandinavian weather allows.

Mushroom Paj

In August, the wild mushrooms start to appear in the Swedish and Norwegian fields and forests. If you are lucky enough to find golden chanterelles, the best thing you can do is fry them in butter and eat them on toasted bread – it is heaven. Where we usually spend time in August, the mushrooms are so plentiful we could eat them morning, noon and night if we wanted to! Another way I use up all the mushrooms is by making this 'paj' – pronounced 'pie', which is actually more like a quiche or a tart.

CHEESE PASTRY

125 g/1⅛ sticks butter, cold and
    cubed
200 g/1½ cups plain/all-purpose flour
50 g/½ cup finely grated Västerbotten
    cheese
¼ teaspoon salt (Västerbotten is salty,
    so adjust if using a different cheese)
1 egg yolk
small dash of chilled water (if needed)
egg white, for brushing

MUSHROOM FILLING

500 g/18 oz. mushrooms (see Note)
25 g/2 tablespoons unsalted butter
1 tablespoon plain/all-purpose flour
2 large shallots
2 sprigs fresh thyme
freshly ground black pepper

EGG FILLING

250 ml/1 cup plus 1 tablespoon
    whole milk
250 ml/1 cup plus 1 tablespoon
    double/heavy cream
3 eggs
freshly grated nutmeg
30–35 g/⅓ cup finely grated
    Västerbotten cheese

25-cm/10-inch loose-based tart pan

baking beans

Makes 1 large tart

In a food processor, briefly blitz the pastry ingredients together to form a dough, adding a tiny bit of chilled water if needed to bring it together. If you don't have a food processor, you can do this by hand by first rubbing the butter into the flour with your fingertips until crumbly, then adding the rest of the ingredients and mixing until smooth. Wrap the pastry in clingfilm/plastic wrap and rest in the fridge for 30 minutes before using.

In a saucepan, dry fry all the mushrooms for several minutes (this concentrates the flavour and avoids too much liquid). Add the butter, flour, onions and thyme and then cook on a low heat with the lid on for 3 minutes. Season with black pepper (not salt at this stage).

Preheat the oven to 200°C (400°F) Gas 6.

Roll out the chilled pastry until nice and thin and use to line the tart pan evenly. Prick the base with a fork a few times, then line the pastry with baking parchment and fill with baking beans. Blind bake in the preheated oven for about 15 minutes. Remove from the oven and immediately brush all over with egg white to seal the crust. Turn the oven temperature down to 160°C (325°F) Gas 3.

Whisk all the egg filling ingredients (apart from the cheese) together and season well. Add the cooked mushrooms (try not to add too much liquid). Pour the egg mix on top, add the grated cheese and bake in the preheated oven for around 30 minutes. Keep the heat low – too hot and the eggs will overcook. Serve for lunch with a leafy green salad and a glass of crisp white wine in the sunshine.

Note: You can choose to just use all chanterelles, but if I'm not in Sweden with a forest in the backyard, then I often mix it up with chestnuts, chanterelles, Karl Johan (porcini), or whatever is available. I sometimes go for a combination of the more expensive flavour-rich dried mushrooms mixed with some cheaper chestnuts (ratio 1:5).

Nettle Soup

Back when I was in primary school, we had to spend time at a Viking centre
to learn about our heritage and history. We had to milk a goat, forage for food
and live in a massive Viking house. The great memories stayed with me, except that
darn nettle soup – something that day made me not like it and I avoided it ever since,
until last year, when I decided to give it another try. It turns out the nettle soup made
by grown-up me is a lot nicer! When I need a vitamin boost, this is now my favourite
soup recipe. Nettles are full of iron and other goodness (google it and you'll see).
There are also plenty of them around! The poached egg and crispy bacon make it extra
delicious, but if you want a veggie version, use vegetable stock and leave out the bacon.

150–175 g/5½-6 oz. fresh nettle tips
   (around a normal grocery
   carrier-bag full)
1 knob/pat of butter
1 onion, chopped
2–3 tablespoons plain/
   all-purpose flour
400–500 ml/1⅔–2 cups chicken stock
50 ml/scant ¼ cup double/heavy
   cream
handful of finely chopped fresh
   chives, plus extra to garnish
2 eggs, for poaching
3–4 thin slices of pancetta
salt and freshly ground black pepper
olive oil or rapeseed oil, to serve

Serves 2

First, wearing protective gloves, discard any thick stems and rough
bits from the nettles. Rinse the leaves and then pop them into a large
saucepan of boiling water for around 2–3 minutes until soft, then
drain. This will kill the stings.

Meanwhile, melt the butter in a saucepan, then add the onion and
cook over a medium heat for 2–3 minutes until translucent. Add
2 tablespoons flour and stir into a thick roux (add the third tablespoon
of flour only if needed). Pour in the warm chicken stock, a little at a
time, and stir into the roux. Keep stirring with each addition and stop
adding stock when you have a nice textured soup that is neither too
thick nor too thin.

Squeeze any excess water from the nettles and roughly chop. Stir into
the soup and leave to simmer, uncovered, for around 15–20 minutes,
then taste and season with salt and pepper.

Pour the soup into a blender or food processor and blitz until
smooth. Return the pan to a low heat, add the cream and season
again. Add the chives, if using, and keep warm on a low heat.

To make the poached eggs, stir a vortex in a pan of boiling water
and crack one egg in. Cook for 3 minutes for a medium-soft poached
egg. Use a slotted spoon to set aside and repeat with the other egg.
Fry the pancetta until crisp in a frying pan/skillet.

Serve the soup in two shallow wide bowls with a poached egg in the
middle of each. Decorate with the crispy pancetta, extra chives and
droplets of good quality olive or rapeseed oil.

Tip: If you don't have enough nettles, add some spinach to bulk it out.

Nettle Crêpes with Ricotta & Green Vegetables

If you don't have nettles, you can make these delicious stuffed crêpes with all spinach instead.

75 g/2⅔ oz. nettle leaves
20 g/⅓ cup spinach
200 g/1½ cups plain/
   all-purpose flour
3 eggs
500 ml/2 cups plus
   2 tablespoons whole milk
handful of fresh flat-leaf
   parsley
freshly grated nutmeg
olive oil, for frying and
   drizzling
sea salt and freshly ground
   black pepper

FILLING
12–15 asparagus spears
300 g/10½ oz. courgette/
   zucchini, spiralized
100 g/⅔ cup fresh peas
200 g/7 oz. ricotta cheese
squeeze of fresh lemon juice
chopped pistachio nuts and
   pea shoots, to serve

*20-cm/8-inch non-stick frying
pan/skillet*

Makes about 8 crêpes

First, wearing protective gloves, discard any thick stems and rough bits from the nettles. Rinse the leaves and then blanch in a large saucepan of boiling water to kill the stings for around 2–3 minutes. Add the spinach for the final minute of blanching. Drain.

Squeeze the excess water from the nettles and spinach, then place in a food processor and pulse. Add the flour, eggs, milk, parsley, salt and pepper and nutmeg. Blend to make a very smooth batter. If you use a stick blender this will give an even smoother result.

Heat a little oil in the frying pan/skillet over a high heat. Add enough batter to just cover the base of the pan. Cook until no longer liquid and small bubbles start to appear, then flip and cook the other side. Keep the cooked crêpes warm in a low oven while you fry the rest, making sure to add more oil for each one.

For the filling, slice your asparagus spears down the middle if quite thick. Blanch the courgettes/zucchini, peas and asparagus in boiling water for no more than 2 minutes, then drain.

To serve, place a crêpe on a plate and add courgettes/zucchini, asparagus, peas and dollops of ricotta. Season well, add a squeeze of lemon juice and scatter with the pistachio nuts. Fold in half, then drizzle with olive oil and decorate with pea shoots.

Västerbotten Cheese Paj

This savoury tart can be found on every Swedish family's dinner table several times a year. It's essential to get hold of Västerbotten cheese as it really does have a very unique taste and it is exported to speciality shops across the world. You can substitute with a good aged Cheddar, but for the 'real' taste, do make this if you have Västerbotten cheese. This one is normally served at room temperature rather than hot, and it is marvellous as part of a summer smörgåsbord or served just on its own with a leafy salad. It is also an essential part of an August crayfish party (see page 95).

PASTRY
125 g/1⅛ sticks butter, cold and cubed
200 g/1½ cups plain/all-purpose flour
pinch of salt
1 egg
small dash chilled water (if needed)

CHEESE FILLING
3 eggs
100 ml/⅓ cup plus 1 tablespoon
   whole milk
250 ml/1 cup plus 1 tablespoon
   double/heavy cream
½ teaspoon paprika
250 g/9 oz. Västerbotten cheese,
   finely grated
salt and freshly ground black pepper

25-cm/10-inch loose-based tart pan

baking beans

Makes 1 large tart

In a food processor, briefly blitz the pastry ingredients together to form a dough, only adding a tiny bit of chilled water if needed to bring it together. If you don't have a food processor, you can do this by rubbing the butter into the flour with your fingertips until it is crumbly, then adding the rest of the ingredients and mixing until smooth. Wrap the pastry in clingfilm/plastic wrap and rest in the fridge for 30 minutes before using.

Preheat the oven to 180°C (350°F) Gas 4.

Roll out the chilled pastry until nice and thin and use to line the tart pan evenly. Prick the base with a fork a few times, then line the pastry with baking parchment and fill with baking beans. Blind bake in the preheated oven for about 12–13 minutes. Remove the beans and baking parchment and bake for a further 5–6 minutes. Remove from the oven but leave the oven on.

For the filling, mix together all the filling ingredients except the cheese, seasoning well with salt and pepper. Evenly scatter the Västerbotten cheese all over the base of the pastry, then pour over the egg mixture.

Return to the oven for about 15–20 minutes. It'll puff up quite a bit towards the end and will turn golden on top. It's done when the middle is set, so do keep an eye on it. Leave to cool before removing from the pan and slicing.

Note: This dish goes very well with romsås, a caviar sauce (pictured). To make this, mix together one small jar of red lumpfish roe with 3 large tablespoons of crème fraîche and leave to set. Just before you serve the tart, stir the romsås again. Alternatively, if you can get real bleak roe (löjrom), serve the tart with a spoonful of this caviar and some crème fraîche and chopped red onion.

Crayfish season

Imagine the scene: a little red cottage by a lake that glimmers in the late summer sunlight. A table in the meadow, decorated with lanterns, bunting or little hats with crayfish on them. Welcome to the crayfish party.

Many moons ago, crayfish were only caught during a specific season in late summer. This came about when a pest nearly wiped out the European crayfish, and for most of the 20th century, catching them was limited to one month of the year. Nowadays, there is no legal issue with catching crayfish, but we Scandinavians do like tradition and most people will still only host crayfish parties during the season – the kräftpremiär – which usually starts the first week in August and lasts for about a month. During this time, most Swedes will attend

quite a few of these crayfish parties – enough to feel that they don't need any more for the rest of the year!

A real crayfish party requires, first and foremost, two things: good friends and crayfish. We usually try to host the parties outside if the weather gods and mosquitoes are kind. A big table is set up and decorated with paper lanterns, crayfish hats and bibs (the bibs are needed as eating crayfish is messy – the hats are just to make everybody look really silly). It's impossible to look good while peeling and eating crayfish, so no need to try.

To prepare crayfish from scratch requires some nerve as you need to cook them live – you can chill them for an hour or so before cooking so they are asleep, if you find this easier. Do rinse each one before cooking. Around 10–12 crayfish per person is about right for the initiated (less for a novice). Don't cook more than a few kilos at a time. Bring a very large pan of water to the boil with some sugar and salt (3 teaspoons of sugar to around 2 kg/4¹/₂ lb. crayfish and around 80–90 g/3 oz. salt) and a few bunches of crown dill (strong-tasting dill that has been allowed to flower). Pour in a bottle of lager or stout and then top up with water. Add the crayfish, making sure they are fully submerged, and cook for about 8–9 minutes, depending on the size. The fish should be cooled in the cooking water, but you need to get it cold fast, so adding the pot to a sink full of ice will help. Refrigerate the fish in the liquid for 24 hours, then serve and eat cold.

Most people these days buy the crayfish ready cooked and frozen. It's a super-easy way to do it – all you need to do is defrost and serve with all the other dishes. It's minimal fuss and doesn't take much effort for the host, apart from clearing up! The dill flavour is the important bit, but you can always add this yourself.

Serve the crayfish in big bowls on the table. They really are the main star of the event and everything else is just filler. At most crayfish parties people will also eat crispbread, crusty bread, cheese and a Västerbotten cheese tart (see page 93) on the side. This is one of those times when the aquavit comes out again, so I always add some salads and maybe some cooked potatoes, just to be safe. I've been to many parties where non-Scandi guests have ended up singing 'Dancing Queen' at the top of their voice whilst declaring their undying love to Ylva from Uppsala. It's a slippery slope.

Beef Lindström Burgers

One of the most famous burgers in Sweden, the biff à la Lindström is named after Henrik Lindström, a prominent industrialist with Swedish parents, who grew up in St Petersburg in Russia. On holidays in Sweden, he taught the chef at his hotel how to make this burger with capers and beetroot/beet. It became a hit across the country – and rightly so as the combination is super-nice. The traditional way of serving these is without the bun and with potatoes on the side. We used to make it like this at home, until my burger-loving kids suggested we add a bun and have it with coleslaw one sunny day. Sometimes, having Anglo-Scandinavian children who are not bound by 'how things are usually done in Scandinavia' means we can find new ways of enjoying old classics. The patties are quite fragile, so be aware of this if you plan to grill them.

500 g/18 oz. minced/ground beef
good pinch of salt
1 onion, finely chopped
100 g/3½ oz. pickled beetroot/beet, finely chopped
40 g/1½ oz. pickled cucumber or gherkins, finely chopped
2 tablespoons capers, roughly chopped
1 medium cooked white potato (approx. 80 g/3 oz.), peeled and roughly mashed
4 egg yolks
1 teaspoon Dijon mustard
salt and freshly ground black pepper
olive oil or rapeseed oil and butter, for frying
4 eggs, to serve

TO SERVE
seeded rye burger buns or buns of your choice, toasted
My Summer Slaw (see page 61)
condiments of your choice

Serves 4

Put the minced/ground beef and salt in a stand mixer with the paddle attachment. Mix for around 1 minute on medium speed. Alternatively, you can mix for a little longer in a large bowl with a wooden spoon.

Add the onion, beetroot/beet, pickled cucumber or gherkins, capers, cooked potato, egg yolks and mustard. Season with salt and black pepper. Mix again until all the ingredients are evenly incorporated (but not too long or the burger will become tough).

Shape the mixture into 4 burgers and leave them to rest for 30 minutes in the fridge before frying.

Preheat the oven to 120°C (250°F) Gas ½.

Heat the oil and butter in a frying pan/skillet. Fry the burgers (in batches if needed, depending on the size of your pan) over a high heat for about 3–4 minutes on each side, depending on how you like your beef to be cooked.

Once cooked, pop the beef patties in the oven to keep warm and fry the eggs sunny-side up in the same frying pan/skillet.

Serve each beef patty on a lightly toasted burger bun with the fried egg on top. Serve with summer slaw and condiments on the side.

Wallenbergare

Swedes love naming dishes after people – I guess it's a good way to keep track
of who liked what! This dish is named after the district council judge Marcus
Wallenberg (1864–1943). Someone in our household misunderstood the name, so in
our family, they are now known as 'Wallanders', after the fictional detective. This dish
is traditionally served with mash and a creamy gravy. However, owing to the sheer
amount of cream in the meat, I like to serve mine with simple boiled new potatoes,
cold stirred lingonberries and fresh green peas. The Hasselback Potatoes (page 108)
are another good serving option. If you do want a gravy, simply use the frying juices.

500 g/18 oz. minced/ground veal
　　(or finely minced/ground pork
　　if you don't eat veal)
1 teaspoon salt
4 egg yolks
dash of soy sauce
250 ml/1 cup double/heavy cream
60 g/1²/₃ cups panko breadcrumbs
　　or other good quality breadcrumbs
a knob/pat of butter, for frying
salt and freshly ground black pepper

COLD STIRRED LINGONBERRIES
150 g/5¹/₂ oz. frozen lingonberries
50-60 g/¹/₄ cup caster/granulated
　　sugar, to taste

Makes 8 Wallenbergare

To make the cold stirred lingonberries, place the frozen lingonberries
in a bowl and stir together with the sugar. Stir every 30 minutes for
a few hours and the sugar will soften the berries. It will be tart, but it's
a great side to meatballs of any kind and it keeps in the fridge for
about a week.

To make the Wallenbergare, add the minced/ground meat and salt
to a stand mixer with the paddle attachment and mix on medium
speed. Alternatively, you can mix in a large bowl with a wooden
spoon. Add the egg yolks and soy sauce and mix until incorporated.
Add the cream in a steady stream and mix until combined. The
mixture will be quite sticky. Put it in the fridge to rest for 30 minutes.

When ready to cook, put the panko breadcrumbs on a plate and
preheat the oven to 120°C (250°F) Gas ¹/₂.

Shape one Wallenbergare at a time, using slightly damp hands,
into small patties about the size of duck eggs. Place in the plate of
breadcrumbs and flatten slightly – the mixture is sticky so the crumbs
will stick well. Turn the patty over and ensure it's covered with
breadcrumbs on both sides.

Heat a knob/pat of butter in a frying pan/skillet until it just browns.
Pop in the pan and fry two or three at a time for 3–4 minutes on each
side – don't overcook or the result will be stodgy and dry. Keep the
coating light brown and crisp and the inside just cooked through.
Transfer to a dish in the preheated low oven to keep warm while you
fry the rest. Repeat with the rest of the meat and breadcrumbs.

Serve the warm Wallenbergare with potatoes, fresh green peas and
a dollop of the cold stirred lingonberries.

Pot Roast Chicken with Parsley

This is an old Danish chicken dish which is traditionally served with baked or new potatoes and agurkesalat (soused cucumber salad). It's food known in Denmark as mormormad – literally: 'grandmother food'. It's the taste of long summer days at her house in the countryside and all the love that never went away.

1 large bunch of fresh flat-leaf parsley
1 whole chicken (around 1.5–1.7 kg/
    3½–3¾ lb.)
coarse sea salt
75 g/¾ stick butter
1 onion, roughly chopped
2–3 bay leaves
10–12 whole peppercorns
new potatoes, to serve (optional)

SOUSED CUCUMBER SALAD
60 g/scant ⅓ cup caster/granulated
    sugar
100 ml/generous ⅓ cup water
100 ml/generous ⅓ cup white wine
    vinegar
2–3 tablespoons finely chopped fresh
    dill (optional)
1 cucumber, thinly sliced with a
    mandoline (if you have one)
salt and freshly ground black pepper

GRAVY
2 tablespoons butter
1 tablespoon plain/all-purpose flour
350–400 ml/1½–¾ cups chicken stock
    (from the roast chicken)
150 ml/½ cup single/light cream
1 teaspoon sugar
dash of gravy browning (optional)
1 teaspoon sugar

Serves 4–5

Take the entire bunch of parsley (reserve a few sprigs for decoration) and stuff into the chicken cavity. Rub the chicken skin all over with the coarse sea salt.

Heat a very large saucepan (with enough room for the chicken and then some) with the butter and brown the chicken skin all over. Fill the pan with water two thirds of the way up. Add the onion, bay leaves and peppercorns. Bring to the boil, cover with a lid and leave to simmer for around 20–25 minutes, before turning the chicken over and cooking for another 10–15 minutes (cooking time depends on the size of the chicken – do check that no pink remains and the juices run clear). When the chicken is cooked, remove from the water and keep warm under foil. Keep the liquid the chicken was cooked in – this will be the stock for your gravy.

Meanwhile, make the soused cucumber salad. Put the sugar, water, vinegar and dill (if using) in a saucepan and bring to a simmer. When the sugar has dissolved, take off the heat and season generously with salt and pepper. Place the cucumber slices in a bowl and top with the liquid. Rest for at least 30 minutes, then drain. If it's too sour, add more sugar. If it's too sweet, add a dash of vinegar. (This salad goes with everything and will keep for 4–5 days in the fridge).

Bring the pan of chicken stock to a full boil and leave to reduce for 10 minutes uncovered. Strain and then set aside in a jug/pitcher.

In a smaller saucepan, melt the butter and then stir in the flour over a medium-high heat to make a small roux. Gradually stir in the chicken stock as you bring the mixture to the boil (the gravy should be quite thin but you may not need all the stock), then simmer for 5–10 minutes. Season with salt and pepper and then add the cream – and sugar, if needed. If you prefer a darker gravy, add a few drops of gravy browning.

If you prefer your chicken skin crispier, pop it under the grill for a few minutes just before serving. Carve the chicken and serve with the parsley, if you wish. Serve with new potatoes, the gravy, soused cucumber salad and summer greens of your choice.

Lena's Danish Meatballs

Lena is my mother. She makes the best meatballs in my world, because, as any Dane knows, mother's meatballs are always the best. Except in my own house, where mormor Lena's are the best, according to my kids. My mother always wins. I am sure that, one day, Danish meatballs will make it as big on the food scene as the Swedish meatballs, which people across the world have come to love. They are delicious, and being larger than the Swedish variety, they don't require as long standing in front of the stove to cook. Most Danes will eat their staple dish of meatballs once a week or so. We eat ours warm with boiled potatoes, gravy and pickled cucumbers (page 102), or cold with potato salad in the summer. We also eat them on open sandwiches and always when we have a kolde bord (the Danish name for smörgåsbord).

300 g/10½ oz. minced/ground veal

200 g/7 oz. minced/ground pork (with a good fat content of around 15%)

1 small teaspoon salt

1 onion, grated

1 UK large/US extra-large egg

3 tablespoons fresh breadcrumbs

1 tablespoon plain/all-purpose flour

1 teaspoon ground allspice

freshly grated nutmeg (optional)

100 ml/generous ⅓ cup warm whole milk with ½ stock cube/bouillon cube dissolved in it

freshly ground black pepper

100 ml/ generous ⅓ cup sparkling water

75 g/¾ stick butter

glug of olive oil, for frying

boiled new potatoes with parsley butter, gravy and Soused Cucumber Salad (see page 102), to serve (optional)

Makes 12–14 meatballs

Put the minced/ground meat and salt in a stand mixer with the paddle attachment. Mix for around 1 minute on medium speed. Alternatively, you can mix for a little longer in a large bowl with a wooden spoon.

Meanwhile, squeeze the excess juice from the grated onion (it does not need to be dry but get rid of most of the liquid). Add the onion to the meat and mix again, then add the egg, breadcrumbs, flour, allspice, nutmeg (if using), milk with dissolved stock/bouillon cube and a good grinding of black pepper. Mix until incorporated. Pop the meatball mixture in the fridge for at least 30 minutes to rest.

Preheat the oven to 120°C (250°F) Gas ½.

Take the meat out of the fridge, then add the sparkling water and mix in. Using a tablespoon, scoop out a quantity of meat mixture the size of a large egg. Use the flat of your hand to help shape the meatballs. Danish meatballs are not round, but slightly oval, like an egg.

In a frying pan/skillet, heat up the butter and leave it to brown and bubble, then add a glug of oil. The quantity of butter is essential for these meatballs, or they just don't get the right crust and flavour.

Fry the meatballs over a medium-high heat, in batches which allow plenty of room for turning, for 2–3 minutes each side. Transfer to the warm oven and repeat until you have used all the meat. Serve with boiled new potatoes, gravy and soused cucumber salad.

Pork Loin with Summer-Herb Crust & Hasselback Potatoes

I love the combination of tarragon and pork – actually, what I love is béarnaise sauce with nearly everything, but it's not the best choice for everyday health. This herb crust contains tarragon, like béarnaise, and it really lifts the flavour. You can add a gravy to make this more of a roast, or serve on a buffet table with a summer salad.

HASSELBACK POTATOES
600 g/1¼ lb. skin-on medium-sized
   new potatoes
50 ml/3½ tablespoons olive oil
1 tablespoon freshly chopped parsley
3 sprigs fresh thyme, picked
25 g/1¾ tablespoons butter, melted
1 garlic clove, chopped
1 teaspoon grated lemon zest
sea salt

SUMMER-HERB CRUST
2 tablespoons finely chopped fresh
   tarragon
2 tablespoons finely chopped fresh dill
3 tablespoons finely chopped fresh
   parsley
50 g/2 oz. finely grated Västerbotten
   or Parmesan cheese
50 g/2 oz. dried breadcrumbs
grated zest of 1 lemon
2–3 tablespoons olive oil

PORK LOIN
2–3 tablespoons plain/all-purpose
   flour
large knob/pat of butter and olive oil
   or rapeseed oil, for frying
1 pork loin fillet (around 500 g/18 oz.)
3 tablespoons Dijon mustard
salt and freshly ground black pepper

cooking thermometer, to test the pork

Serves 4

Preheat the oven to 170°C (350°F) Gas 4.

First, prepare the hasselback potatoes. Using a small sharp knife, make small slices widthways across the top of each potato, reaching two thirds down, to create a fan effect. Place in a large roasting tray.

Mix the oil and herbs together and coat all the potatoes, ensuring the sliced sides face upwards. Roast in the preheated oven for around 20 minutes.

Meanwhile, mix together all the ingredients for the herb crust and put them on a large plate. Put the flour on a separate large plate.

Heat the butter and a glug of oil in a large frying pan/skillet. Sear the pork loin over a high heat until just brown on all sides, then roll lightly in the plate of flour and brush all over with the Dijon mustard. Finally, roll the pork in the herb crust mixture until fully covered.

Remove the tray of potatoes from the oven (leaving it on) and brush them with the melted butter. Sprinkle with the garlic, lemon zest and sea salt. Add the herb-crusted pork loin to the tray, nestled among the potatoes and return to the hot oven for around another 20 minutes until the pork is just cooked through and the herb crust is golden. Use a thermometer to check if you like – I take mine out at 68°C (155°F) and leave it to rest under a foil cover for 10 minutes before slicing. (My husband would take it out earlier, but if I tell you that then we have to have the whole slightly pink-pork debate and that one you can decide for yourself.)

Depending on their size, the potatoes might need a final 5 minutes to crisp up and become fully soft in the middle, but you can leave these in the oven while the pork is resting. Serve the sliced pork and potatoes with gravy as a roast, or as part of a summer buffet table with a selection of salads.

Baked Cod Loin with Samphire

For me, midweek meals need to be fast and easy, even more so in the summer
when I just want to be outside. Cod with mustard, in various guises, is popular all
over Scandinavia. This recipe takes about three minutes to put together, plus oven
time, and you can cook your side dishes while the fish is in the oven. I like plenty of
green stuff to accompany, but others prefer crushed new potatoes with butter and
parsley. Samphire grows on the west coast of Denmark in the salty marshes, and also
along the Norwegian coast all the way to Finnmark, and on Swedish beaches. Oddly,
I hardly ate it when I was living there, but it is so popular in the UK that it has become
a staple part of my diet here. I love it because it is packed full of good stuff and has
hardly any calories. It is quite high in sodium though, so go easy on adding any salt.

200 ml/generous ¾ cup crème fraîche
squeeze of fresh lemon juice, to taste
1 generous teaspoon of wholegrain
   Dijon mustard
600 g/1¼ lb. skinless cod loin
salt and freshly ground black pepper
150 g/5½ oz. samphire

Serves 4

Preheat the oven to 170°C (350°F) Gas 4.

In a bowl, stir together the crème fraîche, a squeeze of lemon juice
and the mustard.

Place the fish in an ovenproof dish and pour the sauce on top.
Bake in the middle of the preheated oven for about 15 minutes until
cooked through. Do check that the fish is white and flaky inside as
the cooking time will vary a bit depending on the size of the fish.

Meanwhile, blanch the samphire for 2 minutes in a large saucepan
of boiling water, then drain.

Divide the samphire between the serving plates and add a portion
of the fish and some sauce on top of each. Season with a little salt
and black pepper to serve.

Tip: For different variations on the sauce, you can replace the mustard
with a bit of horseradish or add parsley if you want a fresher element.

Danish Fried Fish with Remoulade

We have plenty of flat fish in our waters, and we eat a lot of them – either freshly steamed or pan-fried in breadcrumbs with a dollop of remoulade, which is a piccalilli-type mayonnaise that goes with everything. It's the Dane's most treasured condiment.

4–6 fillets of plaice or other flat fish
1 egg, lightly beaten
60 g/1²/₃ cups panko breadcrumbs
olive oil and butter, for frying
chips, salad and lemon wedges,
   to serve (optional)

REMOULADE
50 g/¹/₃ cup finely chopped raw carrots
50 g/¹/₃ cup finely chopped raw
   cauliflower
25 g/scant ¹/₄ cup white cabbage,
   chopped
25 g/scant ¹/₄ cup chopped gherkin
1 tablespoon capers
1 tablespoon chopped shallot
1 teaspoon freshly chopped chives
150 ml/²/₃ cup mayonnaise
100 ml/¹/₃ cup crème fraîche
¹/₂ teaspoon mild curry powder
1 teaspoon ground turmeric
1 teaspoon whole grain mustard
1 teaspoon white wine vinegar
1 teaspoon fresh lemon juice
1 tablespoon icing/confectioners'
   sugar (to taste)
salt and freshly ground black pepper

Serves 4

To make the remoulade sauce, mix all the ingredients together and leave in the fridge for the flavours to mingle for at least 30 minutes before serving. The sauce will keep for around 4–5 days in the fridge. (Note that store-bought remoulade can be much sweeter, so add more sugar if you prefer this version).

Preheat the oven to 100°C (210°F) Gas ¹/₄.

Rinse the fish fillets and pat dry with paper towels. Prepare two wide shallow dishes, with the beaten egg in one and the breadcrumbs in the other. One by one, dip the fish fillets in the egg, then roll in the breadcrumbs to evenly coat, setting aside on another clean tray or dish as you finish.

In a large frying pan/skillet, heat up a good knob/pat of butter and a glug of oil. When hot, add the fish, skin-side down, and fry for 1 minute over a medium heat, then turn over and fry for another 1 minute until cooked through and the breadcrumbs are golden all over. You may need to leave the fish on for a little while longer, do check that it is cooked through by cutting one in half. Fry in batches of 2–3, depending on the size of your pan, and transfer the cooked fish to the warm oven until ready to serve (keeping warm for no more than 15 minutes).

Serve the fried fish with homemade chips, salad and wedges of lemon on the side. Any leftover fish can be enjoyed the day after for lunch on a slice of dark rye bread with more remoulade on top.

cake & fika

We Scandinavians love our coffee breaks.
Pressing pause on the work or chores of the
day to meet for a chat over a cup of coffee
and something sweet – Swedes call this fika.
Fika can be done at work, at home or in cafés
– even a casual fika date is possible. It gives
you the chance to stop, sit down, talk
to people around and enjoy the moment.
Summer is the perfect chance for fika
outdoors, to soak up the warm weather and
enjoy nature's produce outside. This chapter
includes a good variety of bakes, from easy
muffins and cookies to classic Scandi buns,
and layer cakes perfect for celebrating.

Brown Butter & Toffee Cookies

The addition of browned butter changes the whole flavour of these cookies, giving them a rich, nutty edge – they don't last long when I make them for fika at home. I use Fazer's Dumle toffees, which are available in nearly every Nordic shop, or at Scandinavian food stores internationally. They also work well with white chocolate.

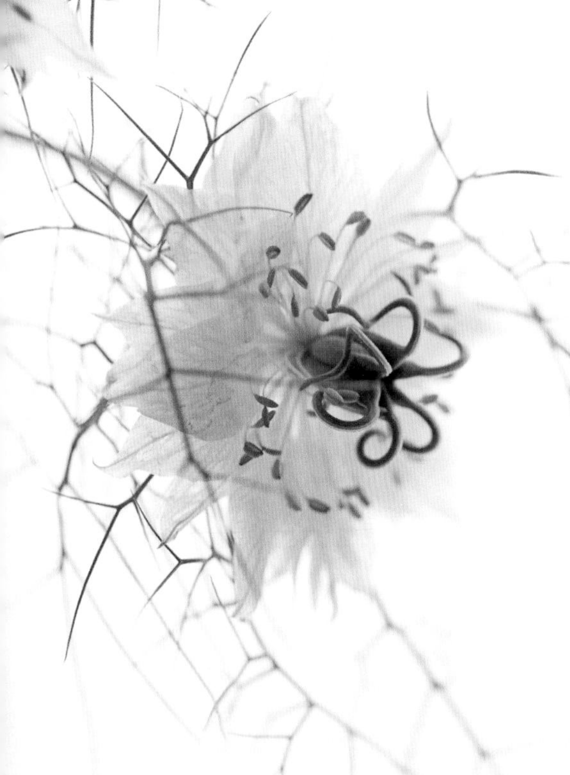

150 g/1¼ sticks unsalted butter
½ teaspoon bicarbonate of soda/baking soda
½ teaspoon mixed spice powder/apple pie spice
300 g/2¼ cups plain/all-purpose flour
½ teaspoon salt
150 g/¾ cup light brown soft sugar
100 g/½ cup caster/granulated sugar
1 egg

1 egg yolk
1 tablespoon maple/corn syrup
3 tablespoons whole milk
2 teaspoons vanilla extract or vanilla sugar
150 g/5½ oz. chocolate-covered toffees (such as Dumle), or white chocolate, chopped
sea salt flakes (optional)

2 baking sheets, lined with non-stick baking parchment

Makes 16 cookies

Melt the butter in a saucepan, over a medium heat until it starts to bubble noisily. Eventually, the bubbles will become smaller and stop. Swirl the pan – you will see and smell the change from yellow butter to brown. Immediately remove from the heat. Transfer to a bowl and leave to cool a little.

In another bowl, sift together the bicarbonate of soda/baking soda, mixed spice/apple pie spice, flour and salt.

Mix both sugars into the browned butter until well incorporated. Add the egg and egg yolk, syrup and milk. Add the dry ingredients, then the toffees or white chocolate and stir to combine. Cover the bowl or wrap the dough in clingfilm/plastic wrap and refrigerate for a few hours.

Preheat the oven to 175°C (350°F) Gas 4.

Form egg-sized rounds of cookie dough using your hands and place on the lined baking sheets. These cookies spread a lot during baking, so leave a minimum of 8 cm/3 inches space between each one. Sprinkle with sea salt flakes, if using. Bake in the preheated oven for around 8 minutes until slightly brown at the sides but not entirely puffed up. Remove from the oven and let cool (if using Dumle, let cool for a bit longer before eating).

Midsummer Strawberry Layer Cake

This is a great cake to make for midsummer or indeed all the way through strawberry season. The whipped cream frosting holds very well in warm weather.

SPONGE

350 g/1¾ cups caster/granulated
    sugar

5 eggs

300 g/2¼ cups plain/all-purpose flour

3 teaspoons baking powder

½ teaspoon salt

100 g/1 cup ground almonds

100 g/1 stick minus 1 tablespoon
    unsalted butter, melted and cooled

1 teaspoon vanilla sugar or
    vanilla extract

100 ml/⅓ cup plus 1 tablespoon
    whole milk

grated zest of 1 lime

WHIPPED CREAM FROSTING

150 g/1¼ sticks unsalted butter,
    room temperature

425 g/3 cups icing/confectioners'
    sugar

2 teaspoons vanilla sugar or seeds
    scraped from 1 vanilla pod/bean

200 ml/scant 1 cup whipping/heavy
    cream

TOPPING/FILLING

½ quantity of Pastry Cream (see
    page 120)

50–70 g/¼ cup raspberry jam

600 g/1¼ lb. strawberries, sliced,
    some left whole for garnish

wild strawberry flowers, to garnish

disposable piping/pastry bag

*3 x 20-cm/8-inch round springform cake
    pans, greased and base-lined*

Serves 10–12

Preheat the oven to 170°C (325°F) Gas 3.

Put the sugar and eggs in the bowl of a stand mixer with the whisk attachment and whisk on high speed until pale and fluffy. Alternatively, you can use a mixing bowl and a hand-held electric whisk.

Sift together the flour, baking powder, salt and ground almonds together and fold into the sugar and eggs until incorporated. Fold in the melted cooled butter, vanilla, whole milk and lime zest until just incorporated.

Divide the batter evenly between the prepared cake pans and bake in the preheated oven for 25–30 minutes until a skewer inserted comes out clean. Leave the cakes to cool in the pans before turning out.

To make the whipped cream frosting, whisk the butter, icing/confectioners' sugar and vanilla on high speed (in a stand mixer or using a hand-held electric whisk) until very well mixed. Add the cream and mix for 3–4 minutes until fluffy. Place in a piping/pastry bag and chill for 30 minutes.

Place the first sponge on a serving plate. Use a palette knife/metal spatula to spread over a thick layer of raspberry jam. Cut a hole in your piping/pastry bag and pipe bulbs of whipped cream frosting spaced evenly around the edge. Fill the inside with a layer of pastry cream and carefully spread out. Add the second layer of cake and repeat, this time adding sliced strawberries on top of the pastry cream, too.

Place the third and final sponge layer on top. This time, don't add jam but repeat the neat bulbs of whipped cream frosting around the top edge and add a nice, thick layer of pastry cream to the middle. Finally, pile on whole and/or halved strawberries, leaving some with their green leaves attached. Add a few wild strawberry flowers, to decorate if you have them.

Summer Berry Tart

The beauty of this tart is in the topping – it showcases everything I love about the Nordic summer: the berries, the sunshine and the abundance of everything fresh.

SWEET SHORTCRUST PASTRY
200 g/1¾ sticks unsalted butter, cold and cubed
350 g/2⅔ cups plain/all-purpose flour
125 g/¾ cup plus 2 tablespoons icing/confectioners' sugar
1 teaspoon vanilla extract or seeds from half a vanilla pod/bean
1 egg

PASTRY CREAM
1 egg yolk
1 whole egg
30 g/generous ¼ cup cornflour/ cornstarch
80 g/⅓ cup plus 1 tablespoon caster/ granulated sugar
¼ teaspoon salt
500 ml/2 cups plus 2 tablespoons whole milk
seeds from 1 vanilla pod/bean
25 g/1¾ tablespoons unsalted butter

TOPPING
600 g/1¼ lb. mixed summer berries such as blackberries, blueberries, wild strawberries, raspberries, cherries or redcurrants
food-safe flowers, to garnish (optional)

25-cm/9-inch loose-based tart pan

baking beans

Serves 8

To make the pastry, rub the cold butter into the flour until sandy in texture, then mix in the icing/confectioners sugar and vanilla. Add the egg and mix until the dough holds together and becomes smooth, taking care not to over-mix. You can also make the dough by pulsing the ingredients together briefly in a food processor, if you like. Roll the dough into a ball, then wrap in clingfilm/plastic wrap and chill in the fridge for at least 30 minutes before using.

For the pastry cream, whisk together the eggs, cornflour/cornstarch, sugar and salt until well combined and set aside. Heat the milk and vanilla seeds until just boiling in a saucepan. Slowly pour one third of the milk into the egg and cornflour/cornstarch mixture, while whisking vigorously to incorporate but not scramble the eggs. Pour the egg mixture back into the saucepan with the rest of the milk. Whisk continuously and bring to the boil again for around 30 seconds until thickened. Remove from the heat and stir in the butter until melted. Pour into a bowl and leave to cool with a layer of baking parchment on top to prevent a skin from forming. Refrigerate, ideally for a few hours, before using. (This pastry cream will keep well in the fridge for a few days, if you want to make it in advance).

Preheat the oven to 175°C (350°F) Gas 4.

On a lightly floured surface, roll out the pastry to 4-5 mm/3/16-¼-inch thick. Carefully transfer to the tart pan. Let the edges hang over (you can trim those after baking). Ensure the pastry is snug in all the curves of the pan, then prick the bottom with a fork all over. Line with baking parchment and baking beans and bake blind in the preheated oven for around 15–20 minutes until golden all over and cooked through. Remove from oven and leave to cool.

Once completely cool, use a sharp knife to trim away any untidy edges while still in the pan. Remove from the tart pan and spread with a generous layer of cold pastry cream. Pile the centre of the tart with fresh berries. Garnish with food-safe flowers, if you like.

Sonny's Sunny Muffins

I have a Swedish friend called Sonny. He's always happy and jolly, he spreads sunshine and joy wherever he goes, and I don't think I've ever seen him in a bad mood. He is one of those people who always has time for others, without expecting anything in return. I made these muffins for him, and they are my version of the traditional lemon and poppy seed flavour.

30 g/¼ cup poppy seeds
50 ml/3½ tablespoons just-boiled hot water
175 g/1⅓ cups plain/all-purpose flour
50 g/½ cup ground almonds (if you prefer them without almonds you can replace this with more flour)
2½ teaspoons baking powder
¼ teaspoon salt
175 g/¾ cup plus 2 tablespoons caster/granulated sugar
175 g/1½ sticks unsalted butter, melted, at room temperature
2 eggs
few drops of vanilla extract
125 ml/¾ cup Greek/plain Greek-style yogurt, at room temperature
grated zest and freshly squeezed juice of ½ lemon

DRIZZLE
50 g/¼ cup caster/granulated sugar
freshly squeezed juice of ½ lemon

12-hole muffin pan lined with 12 paper cases, or 6-hole extra-large muffin pan lined with 6 tulip cases

Makes 6 large tulip or 12 regular-sized muffins

An hour before you start baking, mix the poppy seeds with the hot water and leave to soak. This softens the seeds and brings out their flavour – nobody likes crunchy poppy seeds in their muffins! After an hour, drain and set aside ready to use.

Preheat the oven to 175°C (350°F) Gas 4.

In a mixing bowl, combine the flour, ground almonds, baking powder, salt and sugar and mix well.

In another bowl, mix together the melted butter, eggs, vanilla, yogurt, lemon zest and juice.

Pour the wet ingredients into the dry and fold about 10 times – just enough so that the flour is mixed in. It might be a bit lumpy, but don't worry – trust the power of the muffins! In the last couple of turns, add the soaked poppy seeds.

Pour the batter into your chosen muffin cases and bake in the preheated oven for 10–12 minutes for regular-sized muffins or a little longer until a skewer comes out clean for the larger tulip cases.

Meanwhile, mix together the sugar and lemon juice for the drizzle while the muffins bake.

When the muffins are done, take them out of the oven and prick the tops all over with a fork to make holes. Drizzle over the lemon and sugar mixture and leave in the pan while the drizzle soaks in.

Note: At home, I sometimes like to pipe some store-bought lemon curd (it tends to be firmer than homemade) on top of the muffins just before serving or, indeed, pipe a little inside the centres for a lemony surprise filling).

QUICK RHUBARB & STRAWBERRY COMPOTE

75 g/⅓ cup plus 2 teaspoons caster/
  granulated sugar
2–3 rhubarb stalks, chopped into
  chunks
125 g/4½ oz. strawberries, quartered
squeeze of lime or lemon juice
1 teaspoon freshly chopped mint
  (optional)

SPONGE BASE

100 g/1 stick minus 1 tablespoon
  unsalted butter
75 g/⅓ cup plus 2 teaspoons caster/
  granulated sugar
3 egg yolks
100 g/¾ cup plain/all-purpose flour
  or cake flour
1 teaspoon baking powder
1 teaspoon vanilla sugar or extract or
  the seeds from 1 vanilla pod/bean
60 ml/¼ cup whole milk

MERINGUE LAYER

3 egg whites
pinch of cream of tartar
150 g/¾ cup caster/superfine sugar
50 g/⅔ cup flaked/slivered almonds

TOPPING

100 ml/scant ½ cup whipping/heavy
  cream
¼ quantity of Pastry Cream (see page
  120) (or use 'Kagecreme' powder
  stirred with milk – takes 5 minutes)
fresh strawberries, to decorate
  (optional)

*25-cm/10-inch round springform cake
  pan, lined with baking parchment*

Serves 6–8

Norway Day Cake

I made this for Norway Constitution Day at the café one year and it was a hit. The original Norwegian national cake is called 'Verdens Beste', which means the world's best cake – it's a bold statement, but fitting. In this lighter summery version, I've added a fruity compote, and baked it in two parts instead of all together, which results in a better texture overall.

First, make the compote. Heat the sugar in a saucepan with 3½ tablespoons water for a few minutes until dissolved, then add the rhubarb and stir. Simmer over a medium heat for 4–5 minutes – until tender but not stringy. Take off the heat, and stir in the strawberries. The residual heat will finish cooking the strawberries. Add the lime or lemon juice and mint, if using. This makes more than you need, but you can keep the leftovers in a jar in the fridge for about a week.

Preheat the oven to 175°C (350°F) Gas 4.

For the sponge, in the bowl of a stand mixer (or using a hand-held electric whisk) cream together the butter and sugar with the paddle attachment until pale and fluffy. Add the egg yolks one at a time, beating to ensure they are well incorporated. Sift in the flour, baking powder and vanilla and fold in. Lastly, fold in the milk. Spoon the mixture into the prepared cake pan. Spread evenly and bake in the preheated oven for 10–15 minutes until a skewer inserted comes out clean. Let cool in the pan for 5 minutes before turning out.

In a very clean bowl, whisk the egg whites with the cream of tartar until soft peaks form. Add the sugar very slowly, bit by bit, beating on high speed until stiff peaks form (about 5 minutes). When the cake sponge has cooled a little, remove from the pan and transfer to a cooling rack. Line the base of the pan again with parchment and then spread over the meringue mixture. Lower the oven temperature to 100°C (225°F) Gas ¼. Scatter flaked/slivered almonds on top of the meringue and bake for about 45 minutes. Once cooked, leave in the oven to cool with the door propped open a little bit for 2 hours.

Whip the cream until stiff and fold together with the pastry cream.

To assemble the cake, spread a layer of rhubarb and strawberry compote over the sponge and add chopped fresh strawberries, then a layer of the pastry cream. Carefully top with the meringue layer. Decorate with more fresh strawberries, if desired. I also usually add festive Norwegian flags.

Norway Constitution Day

The Danes and the Swedes both have their national days at the beginning of June, and these are also, of course, celebrated with great pride. However, both the Swedish and Danish celebrations pale in comparison to when the Norwegians gather to mark their Constitution Day in May! It is truly the biggest day of the year for Norwegians across the globe.

There are few dates in the annual calendar as important to Norwegians as 17th May (den syttende mai), when the streets are filled with smiling people, waving flags and overdoing it on strawberries and ice cream. Winter has ended, the last of the snow has melted, even up north, and the sun is (usually) out. The Norwegian fjells are green and fresh, the fjords a majestic and deep blue. Summer is here – and it's time to celebrate Norge.

On this day in 1814, the constitution was signed and independence declared from Sweden. For centuries,

Norway had swung between Swedish and Danish rule – but finally with this day, Norway had begun the journey to full de facto independence. Initially, Norwegians were not allowed to celebrate the day, but by 1833 that had all changed and, over the next few years, the day of national celebration as we know it had cemented itself as the biggest day of the year in Norway.

The 17th May is celebrated by Norwegians worldwide – although the biggest parties, of course, take place in Norway in every city, every town and every village. Across

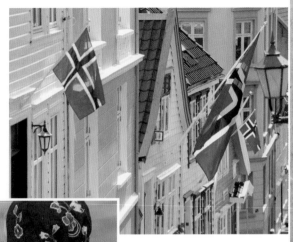

the globe, groups of Norwegians meet up, whether newly emigrated or fifth generation, and host syttende mai celebrations, bringing a piece of Norway to wherever they may be living. London especially has a huge event every year, with a big procession and a day of Norwegian music and food. Many places across the United States, where Norwegians settled over the last century, also still hold this tradition in strong regard.

Families and friends gather early, at around 8am, on syttende mai as there is lots to do throughout the day. A large Champagne breakfast is laid out to fill bellies before the day's festivities at which no expense is spared. It is a koldtbord (Norwegian version of a smörgåsbord) and includes everything from fine salmon to scrambled eggs, air-dried lamb, fenalår (cured lamb), fresh prawns, rømmegrøt (sour cream porridge), and more. This annual koldtbord is treasured by all Norwegians and is likely as big as the Christmas table. This abundance of food sets the tone for the rest of the day.

Both men and women dress up in a 'bunad' (the traditional national dress, that many claim is made from a particular type of extra-itchy wool). Bunad varies from region to region, it is normally decorated with silver buckles and brooches. Once breakfast is finished, everybody takes to the streets to participate in or watch the parades that pass through every town centre. There are red, white and blue flags everywhere and happy kids with rosy cheeks (because, on this day, there is no limit on ice creams, sweets and hotdogs). Meet any Norwegian on this day and you must say 'Gratulerer med dagen' (congratulations for today).

The celebrations continue throughout the day, with more parades, singing of the national anthem and local songs, then speeches, followed by parties. People may continue with dinner at a local restaurant, but many will simply spend the day topping up on fresh strawberries with cream and freshly baked waffles and ice cream. Add more champagne, ad libitum.

Elderflower Everything Cake

This cake is the baking equivalent of denim on denim. Elderflower with elderflower – and then a bit more. It reminds me of Scandinavia and never-ending summer days.

SPONGE

250 g/2¼ sticks unsalted butter, softened
250 g/1¼ cups caster/granulated sugar
4 eggs
175 g/1⅓ cups plain/all-purpose flour
75 g/¾ cup cornflour/cornstarch
2½ teaspoons baking powder
¼ teaspoon salt
grated zest of 1 lime
75 ml/⅓ cup undiluted elderflower cordial (store-bought or see page 168), plus extra for brushing

ELDERFLOWER PASTRY CREAM

3 egg yolks
2 tablespoons cornflour/cornstarch
1 tablespoon caster/granulated sugar
250 ml/1 cup whipping/heavy cream
seeds from ¼ vanilla pod/bean
100 ml/⅓ cup plus 1 tablespoon elderflower cordial (undiluted)
20 g/1½ tablespoons unsalted butter

FROSTING

125 g/¾ cup plus 2 tablespoons icing/confectioners' sugar
180 g/1 cup full-fat cream cheese
50 ml/¼ cup double/heavy cream
grated zest of 1 lime
1 teaspoon vanilla extract
squeeze of fresh lime juice, to taste
washed elderflowers, and/or lime zest, to garnish (optional)

3 x 18-cm/7-inch round cake pans, lined

Serves 10

Preheat the oven to 170°C (340°F) Gas 4.

For the sponge, in the bowl of a stand mixer (or using a hand-held electric whisk) cream together the butter and sugar with the paddle attachment until pale and fluffy. Add the eggs, one at a time, stopping to scrape down the sides of the bowl as needed.

In another bowl, sift together the flour, cornflour/cornstarch, baking powder, salt and zest, then fold into the egg mixture. Lastly, fold in the elderflower cordial until incorporated. Divide the batter between the prepared cake pans and bake in the preheated oven for about 15–20 minutes or until a skewer inserted comes out clean. Leave to cool, then refrigerate (it is easier to naked-frost the cake when cold).

To make the pastry cream, whisk together the egg yolks, cornflour/cornstarch and sugar until well combined and set aside. In a saucepan, heat the cream, vanilla and elderflower cordial until just boiling. Slowly pour one third of the cream into the egg mixture, while whisking vigorously to incorporate. Pour the egg mixture back into the saucepan and whisk continuously while bringing to the boil again for around 30 seconds until thickened. Remove from the heat and stir in the butter. Do taste it – if the cordial you've used is very sweet, then add a bit of lime juice to level out. Leave to cool and then place in the fridge – ideally for a few hours until firm.

To make the frosting, whisk together all the ingredients apart from the lime juice (don't beat the cheese before you add sugar – this can make it runny). Stir in lime juice to taste and chill until firm.

To assemble the cake, put the first sponge layer on your chosen serving plate or cake stand. Brush with a little elderflower cordial, then spread over a layer of pastry cream to cover using a palette knife/metal spatula. Add the second layer and repeat with cordial and pastry cream. Repeat once more with the third layer. For a 'naked' effect, ensure the cakes are lined up exactly and use a flat-edged scraper to scrape some of the frosting around the sides of the cake, then add the rest to the top. This can only work if the frosting is firm and the cake is sturdy enough. If this is not the case, simply add frosting to the top of the cake. Decorate with elderflowers, if in season, and/or some lime zest. Chill until ready to serve.

Summer Fruit Roulade
with Lemon Thyme

In Swedish, we call these 'rulltårta' – literally,
'rolling cake'. I fill mine with pastry cream and any
summer fruits I can find. It's a super-versatile cake.

SPONGE
**120 g/½ cup plus
2 tablespoons caster/
granulated sugar**

4 eggs

**100 g/¾ cup plain/all-
purpose flour**

25 g/¼ cup ground almonds

¼ teaspoon salt

**1¾ tablespoons butter,
melted**

**1 teaspoon vanilla sugar
or extract**

FILLING
1 nectarine or peach

120-g/4½-oz. redcurrants

**20 leaves fresh lemon
thyme, or to taste**

**½ quantity of Pastry Cream
(see page 120)**

**extra red or white currants,
to garnish**

**icing/confectioners' sugar,
to garnish**

*35 x 30 cm/12 x 14-inch Swiss
roll/jelly roll pan, lined with
baking parchment*

Serves 8–10

Preheat the oven to 160°C (325°F) Gas 3.

In a stand mixer, or using a hand-held electric whisk, beat the sugar and
eggs at high speed for around 5–6 minutes until ribbon stage (the whisks
should leave a trail in the mixture when lifted).

Sift together the flour, ground almonds and salt. Fold very gently into the
egg mixture – you want to keep all the air bubbles, as this batter contains
no other raising agent than your carefully created bubbles! Lastly, gently
fold in the melted butter and vanilla.

Pour the cake mixture into the prepared cake pan. Spread evenly and bake
in the preheated oven for about 12–15 minutes or until a skewer inserted
comes out clean. Remove from the oven. To minimise the chance of the
cake cracking, roll it around a clean tea towel when still slightly warm
(leaving the baking parchment on) and allow it to cool this way.

Meanwhile, chop the peach or nectarine into small chunks and mix in a
bowl with the redcurrants and lemon thyme leaves. Place in a sieve/strainer
and leave over a bowl so that the excess liquid can drain away from the fruit.

Once cooled, carefully unroll the cake and spread a layer of pastry cream
evenly over the whole sponge, then spoon the fruit mixture evenly across,
making sure there is a generous amount in what will be the middle of the
roulade. Carefully start rolling the cake tightly around the fruit, using the
baking parchment to help you – ending with the edge of the cake
underneath. Chill until ready to eat. Garnish with more berries and
dust the top with icing/confectioners' sugar just before serving.

Basic Bun Dough

Your classic Scandi bun dough, this can also be used for cinnamon buns.

25 g/1 oz. fresh yeast or 13 g/2½ teaspoons active dried yeast

250 ml/1 cup plus 1 tablespoon whole milk, heated to 36–37°C (97-99°F)

40 g/3¼ tablespoons caster/granulated sugar

80 g/¾ stick unsalted butter, melted and cooled

400–500 g/2¾-3⅔ cups white/strong bread flour

2 teaspoons ground cardamom

1 teaspoon salt

1 egg, beaten

Makes 16 buns

If using fresh yeast, put the warm milk and yeast in the bowl of a stand mixer and stir until dissolved. If using active dried yeast, pour the warm milk into a bowl, then sprinkle over the dried yeast and whisk together. Cover with clingfilm/plastic wrap and leave in a warm place for about 15 minutes to activate and become bubbly. Once activated, pour into the bowl of a stand mixer.

Mix the sugar into the yeasted milk with the dough hook attachment. Once combined, add the cooled melted butter and keep mixing on medium speed for a minute until incorporated.

In a separate bowl, weigh out 400 g/3 cups of the flour and mix together with the cardamom and salt. Start adding the spiced flour to the milk mixture, bit by bit, stirring all the time. When this is all combined, add half the beaten egg (reserve the rest for brushing) and keep kneading for 5 minutes. You may need to add some more flour – you want the mixture to end up a bit sticky, but not so much that it sticks to your finger if you poke it. It is better not to add too much flour as this will result in dry buns.

Once mixed, leave the dough in a bowl and cover with clingfilm/plastic wrap. Allow to rise in a warm place for around 30–40 minutes (or until doubled in size).

Tosca Buns

The classic Swedish tosca topping gives these buns a delicious, nutty caramel crunch.

1 quantity Vanilla Filling from Blueberry & Vanilla Buns (see right)

50 g/½ cup chopped almonds

salt flakes (optional)

TOSCA TOPPING

100 g/1 stick minus 1 tablespoon butter, at room temperature

100 g/1¼ cups flaked/

slivered almonds

80 g/⅓ cup dark brown soft sugar

2 tablespoons plain/all-purpose flour

50 ml/scant ¼ cup double/heavy cream

2 baking sheets, greased and lined with baking parchment

Make the tosca topping while the dough rises for the first time as it is easier to add when cool. Boil the tosca topping ingredients together in a saucepan for 1 minute until thickened. Let cool until needed.

Turn the dough out onto a lightly floured surface and knead through, working in more flour if needed. Roll out the dough to a 40 x 50 cm/16 x 20 inch rectangle.

Spread the vanilla filling evenly all over using a spatula. Scatter over the chopped almonds. Carefully roll the dough lengthways into a long, tight roll. Using a sharp knife, cut into 16 slices and place onto the prepared baking sheets. Leave to rise in a warm place for a further 20 minutes under a clean kitchen cloth.

Preheat the oven to 200°C (400°F) Gas 6.

Brush each bun lightly with reserved beaten egg (from making the dough) and spoon a good amount of tosca topping over each bun – it may spread a bit during baking. Scatter with salt flakes (if using) and bake in the preheated oven for around 10–12 minutes until golden. Watch them as they bake: they can go dark very quickly so you may need to move them around in the oven if they are not baking evenly. Remove from oven and let cool a little before serving.

Blueberry & Vanilla Buns

I use frozen blueberries when I make these buns – too many makes the dough go a bit soggy, but get the perfect balance and they are wonderful.

150 g/5½ oz. frozen
    blueberries
simple sugar syrup, for
    brushing (1 part sugar:
    1 part water – boiled,
    then used warm)

VANILLA FILLING
80 g/¾ stick unsalted
    butter, room
    temperature

1 tablespoons plain/
    all-purpose flour
1 teaspoon vanilla sugar
    or extract, or seeds
    from 1 pod/bean
100 g/½ cup caster/
    granulated sugar

2 baking sheets, greased
and lined with baking
parchment

Turn the dough out onto a lightly floured surface and knead through, working in more flour if needed. Roll out the dough to a 40 x 50 cm/16 x 20 inch rectangle.

Mix together the filling ingredients and spread evenly over the rolled out dough. Scatter the dough with one third of the blueberries. Carefully, fold one third of the dough on top of the other side of the dough and then fold the remaining dough on top of this, so you get a three-layer parcel; around 45–50 cm/18–20 inches long and 12–15 cm/5–6 inches wide. Using a pizza cutter or knife, cut the dough into approx. 16 strips.

Hold one end of a strip with a floured hand, then gently twist the loose end of the dough. Once it starts to entwine on itself, twist the whole strip into a knot, ensuring that the end is tucked underneath. Place on the prepared baking sheets and repeat with the remaining strips. Press the rest of the blueberries into the folds of each bun.

Preheat the oven to 180°C (350°F) Gas 4.

Leave to rise in a warm place for a further 20 minutes under a clean kitchen cloth, then brush with the reserved beaten egg (from making the dough). Bake in the preheated oven for 7–9 minutes until golden. Brush lightly with sugar syrup before serving.

Rhubarb & Custard Buns

In Norway, custard buns are known as 'skoleboller'. I love to make these with added rhubarb – it's such a good combination.

¼ quantity of Pastry
    Cream (see page 120)
2–3 rhubarb sticks,
    chopped into 3-cm/
    1¼-inch pieces
extra caster/granulated
    sugar, for sprinkling
    and rolling

simple sugar syrup, for
    brushing (1 part sugar:
    1 part water – boiled,
    then used warm)

2 baking sheets, greased
and lined with baking
parchment

Turn the dough out onto a lightly floured surface and knead through, working in more flour if needed. Cut into 16 equal pieces, then roll each one into a uniformly round shape and space out on the prepared baking sheets. Cover with a clean kitchen cloth and leave in a warm place to rise for about 10 minutes.

Take a glass or an object with a similar cylindrical shape of approx. 3 cm/1¼ inches wide and dip the end in flour. Press indents in all the buns. Fill each indent with a tablespoon of pastry cream and top with 2–3 pieces of rhubarb.

Leave to rise for a further 15–20 minutes, then brush with the reserved beaten egg (from making the dough) around the edges. Sprinkle a little sugar on the rhubarb (it helps speed up the baking process and ensures the fruit cooks in the time).

Preheat the oven to 180°C (350°F) Gas 4.

Bake the buns in the preheated oven for about 8 minutes until cooked through and golden. Remove from the oven and brush the sides with the warm sugar syrup. Dust the sides in sugar to coat – a bit like a doughnut.

Apricot Tart with Mazarin

Scandinavians use a lot of marzipan in baking, but only the good quality 50% almond kind. It's also really easy to make your own (recipe below). I think apricots are delicious with spice, so I've added cardamom and cinnamon, but omit if you prefer.

1 quantity of Sweet Shortcrust Pastry
   (see page 120)

MARZIPAN
200 g/2 cups finely ground almonds
100 g/¹/₂ cup caster/superfine sugar
100 g/scant ¾ cup icing/
   confectioners' sugar
1 teaspoon almond extract
1 medium egg white, ideally
   pasteurized

MAZARIN
150 g/5¹/₂ oz. marzipan (see recipe
   above or store-bought 50% almond
   content), grated
100 g/¹/₂ cup caster/granulated sugar
100 g/1 stick minus 1 tablespoon
   unsalted butter, softened
2 eggs
50 g/generous ¹/₃ cup plain/
   all-purpose flour
a pinch of salt

TO ASSEMBLE
10 ripe fresh apricots
¹/₂ teaspoon ground cardamom
¹/₂ teaspoon ground cinnamon
icing/confectioners' sugar, for dusting

36 x 13 cm/14 x 5 inch rectangular tart
   pan, greased

Serves 8–10

If making your own marzipan, first re-grind the ground almonds a few times if they feel coarse, as they should be very fine in texture. Blend all the ingredients together in a food processor until smooth. Roll the mixture into a log and wrap tightly in clingfilm/plastic wrap. Chill in the refrigerator for at least 1 hour before using.

Roll out the pastry on a lightly floured surface to a thickness of around 4-5 mm/¹/8-¹/4-inch. Carefully transfer to line the tart pan and let the edges hang over (you can trim those after baking). Ensure the pastry is snug in all the curves of the pan and refrigerate until ready to bake. Freeze any excess pastry for use in another recipe.

Preheat the oven to 180°C (350°F) Gas 4.

To make the mazarin, mix the together the marzipan and sugar until combined, using a stand mixer with the paddle attachment or a wooden spoon, then add the softened butter. Mix again until smooth then add the eggs, one by one, ensuring they are well incorporated. Sift in the flour and salt and fold into the mixture.

Spoon out the mazarin onto the pastry base and spread out evenly. Cut the apricots in half and remove the stones/pits. Arrange the apricot halves evenly across the top of the mazarin. Add a dusting of cardamom and cinnamon and bake the tart in the preheated oven for around 45–50 minutes or until the pastry is nicely browned at the edges and the mazarin has set.

Remove from the oven and allow to cool before trimming away any untidy pastry edges and removing from the pan. Dust with icing/confectioners' sugar and cut into slices. Serve with crème fraîche or sour cream on the side, if you like.

breads

Scandinavian food has many staples –
one of which is our bread. For the perfect
open sandwich, a good rye bread is a must.
For your Midsummer party or breakfast
table, crispbreads are essential. Crusty
rolls for brunch, buns for picnic baskets and
nourishing rolls with added goodness for
lunch boxes. Bread is often given a bad
name, but if you bake it yourself, it has none
of the added bad stuff and provides you with
good, wholesome carbohydrate and energy
for the whole day. Plus, there are few things
as wonderful as a home filled with the smell
of freshly baked bread.

Beetroot & Walnut Buns

I have a thing for beetroot/beet, whether roasted, boiled, raw or pickled. Any shape or form – give this woman some beetroot! I just love the colour of the dough for these buns. The pink colour disappears a little after baking, but the lovely, earthy taste of beetroot/beet remains. I think the walnuts complement the taste perfectly – and I love eating these with some nice aged cheese.

25 g/1 oz. fresh yeast or 13 g/
  2½ teaspoons active dried yeast
400 ml/scant 1¾ cups lukewarm
  water, heated to 36–37°C (97-99°F)
1 tablespoon soft dark brown sugar
200 g/7 oz. finely grated fresh
  beetroot/beet
400–450 g/2¾–3¼ cups white/
  strong bread flour (you might
  not need all of this)
2 teaspoons salt
200 g/1¾ cups wholemeal/
  wholewheat flour
50 g/⅓ cup walnuts, chopped
50 g/⅓ cup sunflower seeds,
  plus extra for sprinkling
milk or beaten egg, for brushing
caraway seeds (optional)

*2 baking sheets, lined with non-stick
  baking parchment*

Makes 16 buns

If using fresh yeast, add the yeast to a stand mixer fitted with the dough hook attachment, then add the lukewarm water. Mix for a minute, then add the brown sugar and stir until dissolved. If using active dried yeast, follow the instructions on the packet – usually you whisk together the lukewarm liquid and yeast in a bowl and leave in a warm place for 15 minutes to activate and become frothy before using. Once activated, pour into the bowl of the stand mixer before stirring in the brown sugar until dissolved.

Add the grated beetroot/beet and allow to mix in. In another bowl, combine the white/strong bread flour and wholemeal/wholewheat flours together with the salt. Slowly add two thirds of the flour mixture to the stand mixer, and allow to mix in on medium speed until incorporated. Add the walnuts and sunflower seeds. If needed, add a little more flour, until the dough comes together – you want a dough that isn't runny, but also not too dry or the buns will be dry. Continue mixing for around 5 minutes in the stand mixer or about 10 minutes if making by hand, until the dough feels elastic.

Cover the bowl with clingfilm/plastic wrap and leave the dough in a warm place to rise for about 1 hour or until doubled in size.

Knead the dough through on a lightly floured surface. Use a sharp knife to cut the dough into 16 equal portions and shape into round buns. Place on the prepared baking sheets and sprinkle with extra sunflower seeds, if you like. Cover with a clean kitchen cloth and leave in a warm place to rise for a further 20 minutes.

Preheat the oven to 180°C (350°F) Gas 4.

Brush the buns with milk or beaten egg. For added zing, sprinkle a few caraway seeds on top just before baking (careful, they're strong stuff). Bake in the preheated oven for around 15–20 minutes or until baked through. Note that baking times will vary a little according to your oven – a good test is to tap the rolls on the bottom, they should sound hollow when done.

Homemade Crispbread

No Scandinavian spread is complete without this.

25 g/1 oz. fresh yeast or 13 g/2½ teaspoons active dried yeast
250 ml/1 cup plus 1 tablespoon lukewarm milk heated to 36–37°C (97-99°F)
2 tablespoons honey or bread syrup
150 g/1¼ cups wholemeal rye flour
300–400 g/2¼-3 cups light rye flour (type 997)
2 teaspoons salt
50–75 g/2–3 oz. seeds, sea salt or spices of your choice, to flavour

pizza stone or 2 baking sheets, lightly greased

Makes 8–16 crispbread

If using fresh yeast, add the yeast and lukewarm milk to the bowl of a stand mixer and stir until dissolved. If using active dried yeast, whisk with the warm milk and leave for 15 minutes in a warm place to activate and become frothy before pouring into the stand mixer.

Add the honey and begin stirring with the dough hook. Mix together the flours and salt. Add about two thirds of the flour slowly and mix for at least 5 minutes on medium speed. If needed, add more flour to bring the dough together. Cover the bowl with clingfilm/plastic wrap and leave to rest in a warm place for around an hour. It will not rise much, but should puff up slightly.

Preheat the oven to a very hot 250°C (475°F) Gas 9. Add a pizza stone if you have one, or baking sheets if not.

Knead the dough through on a floured surface and cut into 8 large or 16 small pieces. Roll each one out onto a piece of baking parchment until very thin.

Push your chosen seeds or toppings into the dough. Brush with water and prick with a fork all over. I usually cut a hole in the middle of mine, too, but it's just for show. Bake in the preheated oven for 4–8 minutes or until golden. Turn halfway through cooking if not using a pizza stone. Remove from oven and allow to cool. Once your oven has cooled to just warm, pop the crispbreads back in the oven for a few hours to finish drying and become properly crisp.

Nettle & Seed Crackers

These little seedy crackers are always a hit in our house. The addition of dried nettles adds a punch of flavour – as well as iron, silicon, and potassium. They are also high in vitamins A and C. I love using fresh nettles, but sometimes it is a faff; luckily dried work well in this recipe.

50 g/5⅔ tablespoons sesame seeds
50 g/⅓ cup flaxseeds (linseeds)
80 g/generous ½ cup sunflower seeds
80 g/generous ½ cup pumpkin seeds
20 g/1½ tablespoons chia seeds
50 g/generous ⅓ cup buckwheat flour
2 large tablespoons dried nettles, plus extra to scatter
pinch of xantham gum
3½ tablespoons cold pressed rapeseed oil or other good olive oil
150 ml/⅔ cup boiling water
¼ teaspoon salt
flaky sea salt, to taste

2 baking sheets, lined with baking parchment

Makes 16–20 crackers

Preheat the oven to 150°C (300°F) Gas 2.

Add all the ingredients (apart from the sea salt and extra nettles) to a bowl and stir well.

Split the mixture in half and place one half on each lined baking sheet. Place another piece of baking parchment on top (sandwiching the mixture) and roll out the mixture thinly and evenly to fit the baking sheet. Remove the paper from the top and scatter with more dried nettles (if you like it stronger) and some flaky sea salt, to taste. Repeat with the second batch of mixture.

Bake in the preheated oven for around 50–60 minutes – do watch the seeds don't brown too much – until completely cooked and dry. I usually turn the oven off and leave in the oven while it cools to ensure they are completely dry. Break into smaller pieces and store in an airtight container.

Carrot & Rye Rolls

My kids love their packed lunches, but giving them some variation in bread for sandwiches is always a challenge. These rolls are a wholesome and tasty option. I find that if you make a batch, then slice and freeze, you can simply take them out of the freezer from frozen, butter and fill, and they will be perfectly defrosted by lunchtime.

250 ml/1 cup buttermilk
  or other soured milk, at room
  temperature
200 ml/generous ¾ cup of
  lukewarm water heated to
  36–37°C (97-99°F)
25 g/1 oz. fresh yeast or 13 g/
  2½ teaspoons active dried yeast
1 teaspoon dark brown soft sugar
4 tablespoons olive oil or
  rapeseed oil
300 g/3 scant cups wholegrain
  rye flour
2 teaspoons salt
50 g/⅓ cup flaxseeds (linseeds)
50 g/⅓ cup pumpkin seeds
50 g/⅓ cup sunflower seeds
100 g/generous ¾ cup finely grated
  carrots
approx. 300 g/2 cups plus
  2 tablespoons white/strong bread
  flour (you might not need all
  of this)
water or beaten egg, for brushing
100 g/¾ cup sunflower seeds, for
  the top of the rolls

*2 baking sheets, lined with non-stick
  baking parchment*

Makes 16 rolls

If using fresh yeast, put the room temperature buttermilk, lukewarm water and yeast in the bowl of a stand mixer and stir to dissolve the yeast. If using active dried yeast, stir together the buttermilk and lukewarm water, then sprinkle over the yeast and leave in a warm place for 15 minutes to activate and become frothy before using. Once activated, pour into the bowl of your stand mixer.

Mixing with the dough hook attachment, add the sugar and oil, then all the rye flour and mix well. Add the salt. Add all the seeds and then the carrots. Slowly start adding the white flour. You may or may not need all of it, depending on how your mixture is looking – it should come together but still be quite sticky and not too dry. Keep kneading for about 5 minutes in the machine, or about 10 minutes if making by hand, until the dough feels elastic and stretchy.

Cover the bowl with clingfilm/plastic wrap or a clean kitchen cloth and leave to rise for at least one hour. (If leaving overnight, use only half of the amount of yeast.) As you are using rye flour, the dough will not quite double in size, but it should rise significantly.

Tip the dough out onto a lightly floured surface and knead it through, working in more flour if needed. Roll out the dough to a rectangle of approx. 30 x 40 cm/12 x 16 inches. Lightly brush the surface with water or beaten egg and scatter sunflower seeds across the surface. Press the seeds gently into the surface of the dough. Using a dough or pizza cutter, cut the rectangle into 16 equal squares and space well apart on the prepared baking sheets. Leave to rise again for about 20 minutes, covered with clingfilm/plastic wrap or a clean kitchen cloth.

Preheat the oven to 180°C (350°F) Gas 4.

Bake in the preheated oven for about 20 minutes or until the rolls are golden and cooked through. (Do check as the cooking time will vary depending on your oven.)

Sourdough Rye Bread

This is my sister's recipe (who got it from someone who got it from someone) and I haven't found a better one yet. The process might seem involved, but a large loaf can keep a family in bread for about a week. Somehow, baking it yourself makes it taste nicer. Ask a baking friend or look up online how to make a sourdough starter. It takes about 5–6 days and you will need a little patience as it can take a few attempts.

DAY 1

4 generous tablespoons sourdough starter (the one you got from your nice friend or make your own)

150 g/scant 1½ cups wholemeal/ wholewheat rye flour

150 ml/⅔ cup room temperature water

DAY 2

300 ml/10½ oz. sourdough starter (made on 'Day 1')

1 litre/4 cups plus 3 tablespoons water

2 tablespoons salt

750 g/7⅓ cups wholemeal/wholewheat rye flour

250 g/1¾ cups white/strong bread flour

DAY 3

500 g/3⅓ cups chopped (kibbled) rye grain

100 g/¾ cup sunflower seeds

100 g/¾ cup flaxseeds (linseeds)

1 tablespoon dark molasses

2 tablespoons barley malt syrup

1 teaspoon barley malt powder (optional)

300 ml/1¼ cups lukewarm water or malt beer

one traditional 1. 8-kg/4-lb. rye bread pan or two small pans, greased (amend baking time for smaller pans)

cooking thermometer

Makes 1 loaf

DAY 1: Mix the sourdough starter with the rye flour and water and leave in a clean sealed jar on your kitchen counter for 12–18 hours. You should see good bubble action and it should grow quite a lot during this time.

Day 2: Drop a teaspoon of your starter mixture (above) in water and check if it floats – if it does, then it is good to go. Mix the rest of the Day 1 starter with the 'Day 2' ingredients in a large mixing bowl. Cover with clingfilm/plastic wrap and leave again on your kitchen counter to rest for 24 hours. Remove 300 ml/10½ oz. of this dough, this will be your sourdough starter for next time. (**Note:** Keep in the fridge in a jar and feed your starter by stirring in a few tablespoons of rye flour and water every few days. Your starter will sit happily in there for a long time – when you want to bake, start from step 1 again.)

Mix the remaining dough with the Day 3 ingredients, ideally for around 10 minutes in a stand mixer with the dough hook attachment, or longer if mixing by hand. The dough will be sticky and gloopy with a texture similar to oatmeal porridge.

Fill the greased baking pan no more than three quarters full with dough. Cover with clingfilm/plastic wrap and leave in a warm place to rise for another 8 hours.

Preheat the oven to the hottest setting, around 250°C (475°F) Gas 9.

Use a fork to prick holes all across the top of the dough. Brush the surface with water, then pop in the preheated oven. Immediately turn the temperature down to 180°C (350°F) Gas 4. Bake for around 1–1½ hours until the internal temperature of the bread reaches 98°C (208°F). Baking times can vary a lot depending on the oven.

Remove the loaf from the pan and cover with a clean, damp kitchen cloth to ensure that no hard crust forms. Once cool, store in clingfilm/plastic wrap to keep the bread soft – leave it at least 24 hours before slicing, as it needs to settle or the inside will be sticky.

desserts & drinks

There is nothing quite as joyful to me as spending a summer evening outside in the garden with a group of good friends, enjoying a leisurely home-cooked meal. By the time the sun is threatening to set in the distance, you might be rounding off the evening with a light dessert, or enjoying a cocktail or two. This is a great example of what we Scandinavians call 'summer hygge' – seemingly perfect moments with no interruptions. Just sharing delicious food and drinks with people you care about, and allowing yourself to appreciate the moment while you're in it.

Birgitte's Buttermilk Panna Cotta with Crunchy Oats & Strawberries

My lovely friend Birgitte is an awesome cook. This is her take on the Danish dessert soup, 'koldskål', also made from buttermilk and vanilla. It's perfect for summer.

8 gelatine leaves
500 ml/2¼ cups single/light cream
2 vanilla pods/beans
140 g/¾ cup minus 2 teaspoons golden caster sugar
grated zest of 2 lemons
600 ml/scant 2½ cups buttermilk
freshly squeezed juice of ½ lemon
250 g/9 oz. strawberries

ALMOND & OAT CRUMBLE
80 g/scant 1 cup jumbo rolled oats
100 g/1¼ cups flaked/slivered almonds
50 g/¼ cup golden caster sugar
50 g/3½ tablespoons butter

4–6 small serving glasses

Serves 4–6

First, soak the gelatine leaves in plenty of cold water to soften.

Meanwhile, pour the cream into a saucepan. Scrape out the vanilla pod/bean and put the whole pod/bean, plus seeds, into the pan. Add the sugar and lemon zest, then gently bring just to the boil over a medium heat while stirring to dissolve the sugar.

Remove from the heat and sieve/strain to remove the vanilla and zest. Bring the cream back to the boil, then remove the pan from the heat again, squeeze out the gelatine leaves and whisk gently into the cream until dissolved. Finally, whisk in the buttermilk and the lemon juice until combined.

Pour the panna cotta mixture into 4–6 small serving glasses. Refrigerate for a minimum of 6 hours – or preferably overnight – until set.

To make the oat crumble, put all the ingredients into a frying pan/skillet and stir continuously for about 5 minutes over a medium heat as the sugar and butter melt – you are aiming for a golden-coloured mixture. The caramelization process happens quickly, so take care not to leave the pan alone or it may burn and taste bitter.

Before serving, cut the strawberries into quarters, leaving the green leaves on some for decoration. Sprinkle the set panna cotta with the almond and oat crumble and top with the fresh strawberries to serve.

Swedish Mess

This is a take on the Swedish Marängsviss, our version of Eton Mess. Marängsviss actually stems from 'meringue Suisse' (Swiss meringue) but the Swedes have adopted the word and made it their own. We've made this for events at the café and it has been a big success. I also make it at home for dessert as it is quick and easy. The combination of hot cloudberry/bakeapple jam/jelly on vanilla cream is just about the best comfort food.

handful of flaked/
  slivered almonds
400 ml/14 oz. good
  quality vanilla ice
  cream
150 ml/²⁄₃ cup whipping/
  heavy cream
1 teaspoon icing/
  confectioners' sugar
3 drops vanilla extract

4 generous tablespoons
  cloudberry/bakeapple
  jam/jelly
4 store-bought meringue
  nests, lightly crushed

*4 dessert glasses or sundae
  glasses*

Serves 4

Lightly toast the flaked/slivered almonds in a dry frying pan/skillet until golden. Stir them often and take care not to burn them. Set aside until needed.

Remove the ice cream from the freezer at this point so that it is easily scoopable. Whisk the cream with the icing/confectioners' sugar and vanilla using a hand-held electric whisk until soft peaks form. Set aside.

Heat the jam/jelly over a low heat in a saucepan or put it in a bowl and give a few short blasts in the microwave until just hot.

Split half of the hot jam/jelly between the four serving glasses, then add one crushed meringue to each glass. Add a spoonful of whipped vanilla cream to each, then divide the ice cream between the glasses, too. Finish with the remaining whipped cream, then the rest of the jam/jelly – and top with the toasted flaked/slivered almonds. Serve immediately.

Pear & Star Anise Trifle

In my first book, I included a recipe for my mother's Danish apple trifle. In Denmark and Norway, it is traditional to use an apple compote layered with different types of fried breadcrumbs and cream. This is another take on that, using pears. Depending on where you live, pears start to be available late summer and through the autumn/fall. I like the hint of anise in the compote – but use ginger if you prefer.

COMPOTE
700 g/1½ lb. just-ripe
  pears, peeled and cut
  into pieces
2 star anise
100 ml/⅓ cup plus
  1 tablespoon water
2 tablespoons caster/
  granulated sugar
1 teaspoon vanilla sugar
  or extract
pinch of salt

BREADCRUMB MIXTURE
3½ tablespoons butter
3¼ tablespoons caster/
  granulated sugar
100 g/scant 1 cup good
  quality dried chunky
  breadcrumbs
300 ml/1¼ cups
  whipping/heavy cream

*4 dessert glasses or sundae
  glasses*

Serves 4

Combine the pears, star anise, water, sugar, vanilla and salt in a saucepan and allow to cook over a medium heat until the pear has broken down and the mixture resembles a compote – around 20 minutes. Set aside to cool down. Remove the star anise when cooled.

To make the breadcrumb mixture, melt the butter in a frying pan/skillet, then add the sugar and mix together. Add the breadcrumbs and stir continuously as they toast to a golden colour.

Whip the cream until stiff.

To your four serving glasses, add a layer of half the pear compote, followed by a layer of half the toasted breadcrumbs. Repeat the layers with the remaining pear and breadcrumbs. Top each dessert with whipped cream. Keep in the fridge until ready to serve.

Rhubarb & Elderflower Crumble with Rye

I like to use elderflower cordial for this recipe, as it means I can make it even when elderflower is not in season! It's a simple twist on the traditional dessert – but the rye adds a unique element too.

500 g/18 oz. rhubarb, chopped
1 tablespoon cornflour/ cornstarch
100 g/½ cup light brown soft sugar
100 ml/⅓ cup plus 1 tablespoon elderflower cordial (store-bought, or see recipe page 168)
seeds from 1 vanilla pod/ bean or 1 teaspoon of vanilla extract

CRUMBLE TOPPING
50 g/⅓ cup hazelnuts
50 g/½ cup rye flakes (or substitute with jumbo rolled oats)
100 g/1 stick minus 1 tablespoon cold butter
100 g/¾ cup plain/ all-purpose flour
100 g/½ cup light brown sugar
pinch of salt

Serves 4

Combine the rhubarb and cornflour/cornstarch in a saucepan and stir. Add the sugar, elderflower cordial and vanilla. Simmer over a medium heat for about 3–4 minutes to start the process of cooking the rhubarb.

Meanwhile, blitz the hazelnuts and rye flakes in a food processor until broken down. Then add the rest of the crumble topping ingredients and blitz again until you have a crumbly mixture.

Preheat the oven to 175°C (350°F) Gas 4.

Put the softened rhubarb into an oven dish, then sprinkle over the crumble topping. Bake in the preheated oven for around 20 minutes or until the fruit is cooked through and the crumble top is golden and crisp. Serve with custard or vanilla ice cream.

Gooseberry Pavlova

Inspired by my parents-in-law, who have lots of gooseberries in the garden of their house near Gothenburg. The tart berries with sweet meringue make a perfect summer dessert.

MERINGUE LAYER
6 egg whites
350 g/1¾ cups caster/superfine sugar
1 teaspoon vanilla sugar or the vanilla
    seeds from 1 pod/bean
2 teaspoons cornflour/cornstarch
a few drops of vinegar

GOOSEBERRY COMPOTE
300 g/10½ oz. fresh gooseberries,
    plus extra to garnish

2–3 tablespoons caster/granulated
    sugar (or more if needed)
dash of water

CREAM TOPPING
½ quantity of Pastry Cream (see page 120)
300 ml/1¼ cups whipping/heavy cream

*baking sheet, lined with non-stick
    baking parchment*

Serves 4–5

Preheat the oven to 120°C (250°F) Gas 1½.

To make the meringue, whip the egg whites in the very clean bowl of a stand mixer or with a hand-held electric whisk until soft peaks form. Start to slowly add the sugar mixed with the vanilla, bit by bit. Continue whisking at high speed for around 4–5 minutes until the meringue is stiff and glossy. If you can no longer feel the sugar grains it is a good indication. Fold in the cornflour/cornstarch and vinegar.

Pile the meringue onto the prepared baking sheet in a loose rectangle shape. Bake in the warm oven for around 1 hour 30 minutes or until crisp on the outside. Turn off the oven but leave the meringue in there to cool for a good few hours if you can, with the door propped open with a wooden spoon.

Prepare the gooseberries by removing the tops and tails. Place into a saucepan with the sugar and a dash of water. Bring to the boil and cook for 3 minutes until the berries are soft. Mash lightly with a fork and taste – they might need more sugar. Gooseberries are delightful because they are sour, so don't add too much. Set the compote aside to cool, then refrigerate until needed.

Whip the cream and fold together with the pastry cream.

Place the meringue on a serving plate and pile over the whipped cream mixture. Top with the gooseberry compote and extra fresh gooseberries to garnish.

Swedish Curd Cake with Raspberries

In Swedish, this is known as 'cheese cake'. If you're looking for one of those sweet American-style cheesecakes, this recipe is not for you. This is a much less sugary, traditional version from Sweden called ostkaka. The recipe first appeared in the 16th-century (yes, it's that old), and the original version requires the cook to make milk curds from scratch using rennet. These days, it's much easier to buy cottage cheese – and that's what I use in my version. Most people use cottage cheese nowadays anyway, apart from purists. I'd say that this curd cake is not dissimilar to the ones you get in the Basque Country– and, like those, it works well with a glass of sweet sherry on the side. This recipe is naturally gluten-free as it has no biscuit base. It is always served lukewarm, never cold or hot. Most people enjoy it with a dollop of strawberry or cloudberry/bakeapple jam/jelly on top and I like it with this raspberry compote.

CURD CAKE
75 g/⅓ cup plus 2 teaspoons caster/
   granulated sugar
3 eggs
400 g/1¾ cups natural cottage cheese
100 ml/scant ½ cup double/heavy
   cream
50 g/½ cup ground almonds
1 teaspoon vanilla sugar or vanilla
   bean paste
pinch of salt
1 teaspoon almond essence (optional)
50 g/⅔ cup flaked/slivered almonds
¼ teaspoon ground cardamom

QUICK RASPBERRY COMPOTE
125 g/4½ oz. raspberries
2 tablespoons caster/granulated sugar
dash of water

*20-cm/8-inch round springform cake
   pan or dish, lined with non-stick
   baking parchment*

Serves 6

Preheat the oven to 160°C (325°F) Gas 3.

Whisk together the sugar and eggs until light and fluffy in a stand mixer or using a hand-held electric whisk. Fold in all the rest of the curd cake ingredients apart from the flaked/slivered almonds and cardamom and pour into your prepared baking pan.

Scatter the flaked/slivered almonds on top, then dust with a tiny bit of cardamom on top – just to give a hint of flavour. Bake in the preheated oven for 30–40 minutes (depending on your oven) until just set in the middle and slightly golden on top.

Meanwhile, make the quick raspberry compote, place 100 g/3½ oz. of the raspberries in a saucepan with the sugar and a dash of water. Boil for about 4–5 minutes until the raspberries have broken down and it looks like a runny jam/jelly. Set aside until needed.

Leave the curd cake to cool to lukewarm (or reheat later to lukewarm) before serving with the cold or warm raspberry compote on top. Use the remaining raspberries to decorate the curd cake.

Vanilla & Cloudberry Ice Cream

In Sweden, we grew up eating warm cloudberry/bakeapple jam/jelly on top of vanilla ice cream. It's simple, but delicious! Making ice cream with the jam/jelly running through it is not so simple, because the sugar content differs between varieties. Using a jam/jelly with a high fruit content and low sugar content is a good rule.

150 g/½ cup cloudberry/
   bakeapple jam/jelly
4 egg yolks
300 ml/1¼ cups double/
   heavy cream
200 ml/scant 1 cup whole
   milk
50 g/¼ cup caster/
   superfine sugar

seeds from ½ vanilla
   pod/bean
pinch of salt (optional)
ice cream machine

Serves 3–4

Sieve/strain the jam/jelly to remove the pips and reserve them for adding at the end if you like.

Whisk together the egg yolks in a large bowl. Set aside.

Combine the cream, milk, sugar and vanilla seeds in a saucepan. Heat over a high heat, stirring occasionally, until just boiling and the sugar has fully dissolved. Slowly pour a quarter of this mixture into the bowl with the beaten egg yolks and whisk vigorously to combine.

Transfer the egg yolk mixture back into the saucepan with the rest of the cream and warm over a gentle heat for 1–2 minutes, whisking, until it starts to thicken and become hot. Do not let it boil or go beyond 70–72°C (158–161°F). Dip a spoon into the mixture – if the back is coated, it's ready. Immediately remove from the heat. Whisk in the jam/jelly. Add a pinch of salt, if needed to balance. Leave to cool, then refrigerate until chilled.

Churn the mixture in the ice cream maker following the manufacturer's instructions. After churning, add the pips back in or fold in frozen cloudberries or extra jam/jelly as you prefer.

Vanilla & Cardamom Ice Cream

If you don't like cardamom and lemon in your ice cream, just leave it out and you'll have a nice vanilla ice cream. If you prefer a heavier cardamom flavour, leave out the lemon.

4 egg yolks
400 ml/1²/₃ cups double/ heavy cream
100 ml/¹/₃ cup plus 1 tablespoon whole milk
80 g/¹/₃ cup plus 1 tablespoon caster/ superfine sugar
seeds from 1 vanilla pod/ bean
10 cardamom seeds (around 3 pods), crushed and finely ground (remove any larger bits of husk)
grated zest from ½ lemon (reserve the juice)
ice cream machine

Serves 3–4

Whisk together the egg yolks in a large bowl. Set aside.

Combine the cream, milk, sugar and vanilla seeds in a saucepan. Heat over a high heat, stirring occasionally, until just boiling and the sugar has fully dissolved. Slowly pour a quarter of this mixture into the bowl with the beaten egg yolks and whisk vigorously to combine.

Transfer the egg yolk mixture back into the saucepan with the rest of the cream and warm over a gentle heat for 1–2 minutes, whisking, until it starts to thicken and become hot. Do not let it boil or go beyond 70–72°C (158–161°F). Dip a spoon into the mixture – if the back is coated it's ready. Immediately remove from the heat.

Whisk in the crushed cardamom and lemon zest – and then leave to cool down a bit before whisking in 2 tablespoons of lemon juice. Leave to cool completely, then refrigerate until chilled.

Churn the mixture in the ice cream maker following the manufacturer's instructions.

Liquorice Ice Cream

Most Nordic people have a big thing for liquorice. Some say that it stems from our food heritage and the fact that our ancestors ate a lot of salted foods. It's certainly also because we tend to be introduced to it at a young age. Once you acquire the taste for it, you never really lose it!

4 egg yolks
400 ml/1²/₃ cups double/ heavy cream
100 ml/¹/₃ cup plus 1 tablespoon whole milk
80 g/ ¹/₃ cup plus 1 tablespoon caster/ superfine sugar
1 tablespoon liquorice power (I use Lakrids raw liquorice powder), plus extra or liquorice syrup, to serve
ice cream machine

Serves 3–4

Whisk together the egg yolks in a large bowl. Set aside.

Combine the cream, milk and sugar in a saucepan. Heat over a high heat, stirring occasionally, until just boiling and the sugar has fully dissolved. Slowly pour a quarter of this mixture into the bowl with the beaten egg yolks and whisk vigorously to combine.

Transfer the egg yolk mixture back into the saucepan with the rest of the cream and warm over a gentle heat for 1–2 minutes, whisking, until it starts to thicken and become hot. Do not let it boil or go beyond 70–72°C (158–161°F). Dip a spoon into the mixture – if the back is coated it's ready. Immediately remove from the heat.

Whisk in the liquorice powder and stir until dissolved Leave to cool completely, then refrigerate until chilled. Do taste as you go – everybody's liquorice tolerance is different and a Scandi person may well need more liquorice than someone not used to the flavour.

Churn the mixture in the ice cream maker following the manufacturer's instructions. Before serving, dress with liquorice syrup or more liquorice powder.

Easy Elderflower Cordial

The season for fresh elderflowers doesn't last too long. If you are lucky enough to have a tree in your garden (or if, like me, you have nice neighbours with overgrown trees) do make the most of the season with this delicious cordial. Some people like it strong, some like it weak, and some prefer it in a cocktail– so dilute, mix and use to taste.

40 heads of fresh
    elderflower, in bloom
2 lemons (unwaxed)
1 lime (unwaxed)
1.5 litres/2 pints water
1 kg/2¼ lb. caster/
    superfine sugar
50 g/1¾ oz. citric acid
    (available online)

*very large saucepan
(around a 3 litre/5 pint
capacity)*

muslin/cheesecloth

sterilized glass bottles

*Makes about 1 litre/
1¾ pints*

Check the flower heads for bugs first (you can give them a quick rinse and shake if you prefer), then place in your very large saucepan. Wash the lemons and lime and cut into slices, then add to the pan with the flowers. Set aside for a moment.

In a separate saucepan, boil the water and the sugar together just to allow the sugar to dissolve, then stir in the citric acid. Pour this hot syrup over the flowers in the large pan and stir. Cover and simply leave to infuse for around 2–3 days, ideally in the fridge or somewhere quite cold.

Sieve/strain the liquid through a muslin/cheesecloth or even a very clean kitchen cloth (discarding all the flowers and bits). Pour into bottles and keep cold. If you sterilize the bottles first (I run mine through a very hot dishwasher), your cordial will keep for many months unopened in the fridge. If you plan to use within a week, simply keep cold and use up. Dilute to taste to serve.

Annika's Rhubarb Drink

My Swedish sister-in-law Annika makes this lovely juice in the summer months when the rhubarb goes mad in the garden and we all desperately try to find ways to benefit from all the goodness before it's too late. This is not a cordial, but just a great way to use up a glut of rhubarb. I've been known to add a dash of vodka and a slice of lemon for a more grown-up version.

1 kg/2¼ lb. rhubarb
1 litre/1¾ pints of water
350 g/1¾ cups caster/
    superfine sugar
freshly squeezed juice of
    1½ lemons, or more if
    needed

4 whole cardamom pods
    (or 1 vanilla pod/bean)

muslin/cheesecloth

sterilized glass bottles

*Makes about 1.15 litres/
2 pints*

Cut the rhubarb into roughly 2.5-cm/1-inch pieces (no need to be neat about this). Place in a large saucepan with the water and bring to the boil. Simmer for 20 minutes. Don't stir it, just leave it to bubble.

Sieve/strain the rhubarb through muslin/cheesecloth, collecting the juices in a new bowl. Don't touch the fruit, don't push it through – just let the liquid come through on its own until it stops dripping.

Transfer the collected juices back into the saucepan on the stove and discard the fruit pulp. Add the sugar, lemon juice and cardamom or vanilla to the pan. Note that rhubarb juice can be quite sickly if you don't add enough acidity, so be generous with the lemon juice.

Bring back to the boil and stir a little to allow the sugar to melt completely, then turn off the heat and leave to cool. If needed, pour through a sieve/strainer again to remove any bits of spices or fruit. Decant into sterilized glass bottles and keep in the fridge for up to a week. Dilute to taste to serve.

Homemade Aquavit

Aquavit is a flavoured, alcoholic spirit to enjoy with your smörgåsbord. Dill, caraway and fennel are common flavourings, but berries or flowers can be used too. Purists would use an aquavit base like Brøndums, but vodka is much easier to get hold of outside Scandinavia.

DILL AQUAVIT
1 bunch of fresh dill
1 teaspoon white sugar
350 ml/1½ cups vodka, plus
   extra to taste

*large sterilized mason/kilner
jar and glass bottle*

coffee filter

FENNEL AQUAVIT
½ fennel bulb, chopped
   into 4–6 pieces
1 teaspoon white sugar
350 ml/1½ cups vodka,
   plus extra to taste

*large sterilized mason/kilner
jar and glass bottle*

coffee filter

*Makes
around
350 ml/12 fl oz.
each dill or
fennel aquavit*

For the dill aquavit, blanch the dill in boiling water for a few seconds, then shake dry and add to the jar (I would always blanch fresh herbs before adding as it gives a stronger taste). Add the sugar, then top up with vodka and stir. Seal the jar and leave for 5–6 days at room temperature. Strain through the coffee filter to remove the dill. Decant into the new bottle and keep for another month before topping up with more vodka to taste. Serve chilled in shot glasses.

For fennel aquavit, put the fennel in the jar, add the sugar, top up with vodka and stir. Seal and leave at room temperature for 2–3 weeks. Strain through the coffee filter to remove the fennel. Decant into the new bottle and top up with more vodka to taste. This makes a yellow aquavit that tastes a bit like ouzo. Serve chilled in shot glasses.

Jon Anders Fjeldsrud's Aquavit Cocktails

We're good friends with a guy who's an expert on aquavit. Not a bad friend to have, you know, when you are a Scandi aquavit-loving person. Jon is a regular at the café, where he hosts aquavit classes and teaches us all about the complex nature of our favourite tipple. He also happens to be a mean cocktail maker, and often makes really delicious aquavit concoctions like these.

Jon's Bloody Mary

Making cocktails with aquavit is great fun, because lots of traditional cocktails can work with it. However, because of the strong flavour notes, you need to adjust the mixers slightly. This Bloody Mary uses dill-flavoured aquavit (see page 171), which brings a fresh lift to the tomato juice. We sometimes serve this for weekend brunch at the café.

2½ tablespoons Dill
   Aquavit (store-bought
   or see recipe page 171)
100 ml/⅓ cup plus
   1 tablespoon tomato
   juice
2 teaspoons fresh lemon
   juice
pinch of salt and black
   pepper
pinch of celery salt
3 dashes of Tabasco
   Sauce

3 dashes of
   Worcestershire Sauce
3 dashes of Maggi sauce
   (optional)
1 teaspoon dry sherry
1 teaspoon red wine
½ teaspoon orange juice
celery stalk or slice of
   cucumber and fresh
   dill sprig, to garnish
   (optional)

Serves 1

Stir all the ingredients in a mixing glass with ice for 30 seconds. Strain into a highball glass over ice. Add your chosen garnish, whether a celery stalk, slice of cucumber and/or a sprig of fresh dill. Serve immediately.

Lola's Burns Martini

This is Jon's go-to Friday after-work cocktail. It's so easy – simply stir the ingredients together and serve over ice. There is just something great about starting the weekend drinking from a martini glass while enjoying the early evening sun.

3½ tablespoons
   OP Anderson aquavit
3½ tablespoons Dolin
   sweet white vermouth
grapefruit zest,
   to garnish

Serves 1

Add the ingredients to a mixing glass over ice and stir. Pour into a chilled martini glass. Squeeze the grapefruit zest over the drink to express the citrus oils into the glass, then drop into the drink. Serve immediately.

Index

Acknowledgments

Thank you to my people, Astrid, Elsa and Jonas Aurell.

Thank you to Ryland Peters & Small and the wonderful team who worked on this book: Julia Charles, Cindy Richards, Sonya Nathoo and Alice Sambrook. Pete Cassidy, Tony Hutchinson, Kathy Kordalis, Casey Lazonik, Sarah Fassnidge and Liberty Fennell.

To David Jørgensen, always and forever with the red pen and nice words.

To my agents, Jane Graham Maw and Vivienne Clore.

Thank you Birgitte Agger Mote for your support and brilliant recipe contribution (I look forward to your book one day). Jon Anders Fjeldsrud for your aquavit wisdom and delicious cocktail recipes.

Everyone at ScandiKitchen who make it happen every single day – with an extra-special thank you to Rebekka, Martina and Live.

The biggest thank you of all to our wonderful customers who pop by and see us at the café, or who contact us from all corners of the world: you guys make what we do worthwhile and we are humbled to share our journey with you.